Painting Baby Animals

WITH PEGGY HARRIS

Painting Baby Animals

WITH PEGGY HARRIS

NORTH LIGHT BOOKS
CINCINNATI, OHIO

Painting Baby Animals With Peggy Harris. Copyright ©
1996 by Peggy Harris. Manufactured in China. All rights re-
served. No part of this book may be reproduced in any form
or by any electronic or mechanical means including informa-
tion storage and retrieval systems without permission in
writing from the publisher, except by a reviewer, who may
quote brief passages in a review. Published by North Light
Books, an imprint of F&W Publications, Inc., 1507 Dana Ave-
nue, Cincinnati, Ohio 45207. (800) 289-0963. First edition.

Other fine North Light Books are available from your local
bookstore, art supply store or direct from the publisher.

03 02 01 00   6 5 4 3

Library of Congress Cataloging-in-Publication Data

Harris, Peggy.
    Painting baby animals with Peggy Harris / Peggy Harris.
        p. cm.
    Includes index.
    ISBN 0-89134-719-4 (pbk. : alk. paper)
    1. Animals in art. 2. Animals—Infancy—Pictorial works.
    3. Painting—Technique. I. Title.
ND1380.H37 1996
751.45′432—dc20   96-1778
                                                     CIP

Edited by Kathy Kipp
Production Editor: Amy Jeynes
Designed by Sandy Conopeotis Kent

METRIC CONVERSION CHART		
TO CONVERT	**TO**	**MULTIPLY BY**
Inches	Centimeters	2.54
Centimeters	Inches	0.4
Feet	Centimeters	30.5
Centimeters	Feet	0.03
Yards	Meters	0.9
Meters	Yards	1.1
Sq. Inches	Sq. Centimeters	6.45
Sq. Centimeters	Sq. Inches	0.16
Sq. Feet	Sq. Meters	0.09
Sq. Meters	Sq. Feet	10.8
Sq. Yards	Sq. Meters	0.8
Sq. Meters	Sq. Yards	1.2
Pounds	Kilograms	0.45
Kilograms	Pounds	2.2
Ounces	Grams	28.4
Grams	Ounces	0.04

About the Artist

PEGGY HARRIS was born in Washington, DC, and raised in Leawood, Kansas. It was obvious from childhood that Peggy was gifted in art. At a very early age, she began studying at the Kansas City Art Institute. Her studies continued through college, and she graduated from the University of Kansas.

After her marriage to her husband, Bob, Peggy took a hiatus from her art. Peggy and Bob traveled extensively throughout the United States and abroad, and after settling in Nashville, Tennessee, began raising their daughter, Kathy.

Soon, Peggy resumed her painting and began to concentrate on her favorite subject and lifelong love . . . baby animals. She developed her now-trademark "halo" background, a style inspired by the method, often taught to children, of "putting a pinhole in a file card and peering through it to really 'see' the baby animal, but still not disturb its privacy."

Peggy's paintings were an immediate hit! Fans and collectors quickly grew from the hundreds to the thousands. To supply the demand, Peggy began to experiment with various mediums, canvases, brushes and tools . . . the right combination of which would allow her to achieve a high-quality painting with the soft, furry look she envisioned, in a modicum of time. Her discoveries culminated in "The Harris Method," which yields "The Harris Look"—all of which is described in depth in this book. In eighteen years, incredibly, thousands of paintings have flowed from Peggy's easel, all of which have sold to collectors nationally and internationally . . . many of whom reach out to touch the painting to see if they can "feel the fur."

The sheer number of Peggy's paintings and the obvious appeal of her designs were not lost on WDCN-Nashville, which developed a television series around Peggy and her method. Today, *Peggy Harris' Paintable Kingdom*, a production of WDCN-Nashville—complete with Peggy's friendly, encouraging voice, her "You *can* do it!" attitude, her sparkling eyes and smile, and her familiar ruffled blue painting shirt—is enjoyed by legions of fans on public television stations nationwide.

Now . . . from her studio in the wooded hills of middle Tennessee, surrounded by pets and wildlife alike, Peggy invites you to join her in appreciating the innocence, joy, wonder and beauty of one of nature's greatest gifts . . . baby animals!

Table of Contents

Peggy's No-Fail Painting Method

Painting Baby Animals With Peggy Harris opens a whole new world of fast and fun techniques for painting amazingly realistic fur and feathers. Now you, too, can create animals you'll want to reach out and touch.

What makes these techniques so special? They combine the use of exposed bare canvas for "whites" with a transparentizing medium ("GEL"), a "scrumbled" paint pattern, cotton balls and Q-Tips, and a stiff bristle brush to create glowing, lifelike baby animals. Even beginners can create magical shading and effortless three-dimensional effects. Best of all, it's no-fail painting. The wet-on-wet oil paint method allows you to change and perfect your painting over and over.

If you love animals, use this book as a starting point to explore your own creativity. You may want to paint these baby animals just as they are in the paintings, or change them with your own personal touches. Perhaps you'll use this method to paint your own pet from a photo. You may even use the techniques to paint a giant grizzly bear. The possibilities are endless if you keep painting, have fun, and try new subjects, techniques and styles. Keep what works for *you* . . . make it *yours!*

MATERIALS

Getting started in *Painting Baby Animals* is relatively inexpensive. Small canvases, a limited palette of oil paints, and everyday "fluff stuff" that you probably already have around the house—all let you achieve maximum success with minimum outlay.

As with any artistic endeavor, good tools more than pay for themselves. Since you don't have to buy quantity, go for quality . . . especially when choosing brushes!

Everything You'll Need to Start

1 *Easel* or slanted drawing board

2 *Canvas* smooth or "portrait" grade canvas, by the roll or pad, cut to 10¾" × 12¾"

3 *Masking Tape* 1½" width

4 *Transfer Materials* tracing or wax paper —heavy coated paper or card stock for stencils —graphite paper (optional)

5 *Stylus* or *Pen*

6 *Turp Can* small pet food can

7 *Small Palette* small plate or cut-down plastic lid from Q-Tip box

8 *Palette Knife* small painting knife

9 *Brushes* *Must have*: 1. tiny sable (or soft hair) round, 2. small sable (or soft hair) bright, 3. medium sable (or soft hair) bright, 4. professional-quality stiff, white bristle rounds (sizes 1 and 2 preferred), 5. small soft hair fan brush (for Projects 8 and 9)

10 *Oil Paints* 1. Titanium White, 2. Ivory Black, 3. Raw Umber, 4. Cadmium Yellow Light, 5. Burnt Sienna, 6. Sap Green, 7. Red (Vermilion or any bright red), small size, 8. Prussian Blue, small size

11 *Linseed Oil* small (for Project 11)

12 *Cobalt Drier* optional

13 *Artists' Odorless Thinner*

14 *GEL* Martin/F. Weber Res-n-gel Quick Drying Extender Gel (new, nontoxic) or Grumbacher Gel Transparentizer Artists' Oil Medium

NOTE: *Both gel mediums transparentize and hold fur brushmarks equally well. Paintings using Res-n-gel will be dry to the touch within twenty-four hours and will retain a soft sheen, making varnishing less critical. Grumbacher GEL is slower to dry and is useful in backgrounds that must be wet for longer periods of time.*

GEL Substitutions: *Other products may be substituted with some adjustments and varying results if the above gel mediums are not available.*

For Backgrounds—Replace turpy gel medium with a tiny amount of linseed oil rubbed on the canvas with a cotton ball before the paint is applied.

For Fur—Replace gel medium with minimal amounts of thickened linseed oil or experiment with synthetic resin mediums that don't dry too fast.

15 *"Fluff Stuff"* Chesebrough-Pond's Q-Tips Cotton Swabs, 300 count or more preferred —Paper towels (soft and heavy) —Cotton balls (plastic-bagged "cosmetic puffs")

16 *X-Acto Knife* with a #11 blade

17 *Picture Varnish* optional

What Peggy Uses

Before you begin, check the materials list for each project. Individual projects will require fewer colors and brushes than shown above. You may wish to begin with only four brushes and add to your collection gradually. Buy less—buy better!

Materials vary greatly from one manufacturer to the next. You may find it helpful to compare your supplies to these particular supplies that were used to create the baby animals in this book.

Canvas—Fredrix Artists' Canvas #10982 Ultrasmooth, sold off the roll. (Fredrix "It's the Real Thing" canvas pads may be substituted. They're not quite as smooth, but they're close enough.)

GEL—Grumbacher GEL Transparentizer Medium, Res-n-gel Extender Gel Medium

Oil Paint—Grumbacher Pre-tested Artists' Oil Colors

Mediums—Linseed oil, cobalt drier, artists' odorless thinner

Brushes—Professional-quality stiff, white bristles (Rounds) Sizes 1, 2

—Grumbacher Renoir Series 100% red sable #626R (Rounds) Sizes 0, 1

—Grumbacher Renoir Series 100% red sable #626B (Brights) Sizes 1, 2, 3, 4, 5

Fluff Stuff—Chesebrough-Ponds' Q-Tips Cotton Swabs, 300 count or more

—Viva Job Squad paper towels

—Generic brands of rayon or cotton cosmetic puffs

Picture Varnish—Grumbacher 100% Damar Gloss Spray

White Acrylic Paint—covers any small dark specks on exposed canvas areas outside the grey halo. Lightly touch them up after the painting is dry and before it is varnished.

MIXING YOUR COLORS

These are approximate formulas based on Grumbacher Pre-tested Oil Colors. Since oil colors vary greatly in staining power according to the brand used, be sure to match your colors to the colors in the pictures. When mixing, begin with the first color and gradually add successive colors until you achieve the correct shade.

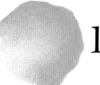

1 *Background Grey*
8 parts Titanium White
1 part Ivory Black

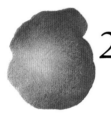

2 *Fawn*
2 parts Cadmium Yellow Light
1 part Burnt Sienna
1 part Raw Umber
(Use less yellow for a deep fawn color)

3 *Grass Green*
5 parts Sap Green
1 part Raw Umber

4 *Deep Yellow-Orange*
Cadmium Yellow Light with a touch of red

5 *Deep Yellow*
Cadmium Yellow Light with a touch of Burnt Sienna and red

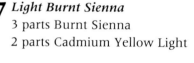

6 *GEL'ed Yellow*
3 to 4 parts GEL medium
1 part Cadmium Yellow Light

7 *Light Burnt Sienna*
3 parts Burnt Sienna
2 parts Cadmium Yellow Light

8 *Medium Blue*
6 parts Titanium White
2 parts Ivory Black
1 part Prussian Blue

9 *Dark Blue*
3 parts Titanium White
2 parts Ivory Black
1 part Prussian Blue

10 *Blue-Green*
6 parts Sap Green
1 part Prussian Blue

28 TERMS TO KNOW

1 *Airplane* To lift off of or come down on the canvas with the Q-Tip or paint brush, gradually and smoothly, as if it were an airplane and the canvas the runway.

2 *Bright brush* A type of brush that has a flat ferrule and a square, chiseled-looking tip.

3 *Bristle brush* A stiff bristle brush. Synthetic bristle brushes work well in this technique.

4 *Dirt (Dirty)* Unwanted paint deposited in white areas of the canvas by lift-out tools. Also, paint that has accumulated in these tools and is apt to be redeposited in unwanted areas.

5 *Dry Q-Tip* A fresh Q-Tip that has no turp or paint in it.

6 *Fall off or Flow off (the brush)* Allowing thinned paint to flow from the brush to the painting surface without letting the hairs of the brush touch the underlying paint or the surface of the canvas.

7 *GEL* Solidified linseed oil medium from Grumbacher. Substitutions require some alteration of technique. Results may vary. (See page 8.)

8 *Glow* To create the illusion of light on an area by lifting out paint with a turped Q-Tip or turp brush. —Dry-glow: To create a subtler highlight area by lifting out paint with a dry Q-Tip.

9 *Float* To place paint on top of paint without disturbing the previous layer.

10 *Layer (fur)* To brush a line of fur using existing paint, wrapping it over and around the animal's body. Also, to brush one fur layer overlapping another.

11 *Lift out* To remove paint from the canvas with a paper towel, cotton ball, Q-Tip or brush.

12 *Perpendicular brush* A brush held with its handle at a right angle to the canvas and with all the bristle tips touching the canvas.

13 *Puddle* Letting a droplet of paint flow from the brush onto the middle of a shape and then stretching it to the correct size and shape by stirring it with the brush.

14 *Re-brush* To perfect a previously brushed area of fur with a bristle brush. Usually refers to brushing an area that has been glowed.

15 *Rotation (of fur)* Brushing fur in an orderly sequence of angles as it radiates out from a central point.

16 *Rough-brush* To brush layers of fur on an image using a bristle brush to blend the paint pattern.

17 *Round brush* A type of brush that has a round ferrule and a pointed tip. Comes in both hair and bristle brushes.

18 *Scrumble* Invented word meaning a "scruffy-jumble" of paint used in the paint pattern. Usually implies large S-shaped strokes and/or squiggles, loosely applied.

19 *Shield* A piece of heavy coated paper placed over areas of the painting to protect it from paint smears and other damage as you work. A shield may be shaped to allow maximum exposure of the image.

20 *Snowplow* To destroy the effect of delicate fur tips by brushing excess paint into the tips. Caused by not airplaning the brush.

21 *Sticky paint* Paint used directly as it comes from the tube, with no thinning.

22 *Stipple (Splat)* To tap the brush rapidly in an area with the brush held perpendicular to the canvas. "Splat" implies stippling with hard hits that cause the bristles to splay.

23 *Travel color* To allow color accumulated in the bristle brush while brushing fur to be deposited in unwanted areas.

24 *Turp* Artists' odorless thinner or artists' grade turpentine.

25 *Turp brush* A small- or medium-sized bright sable (or hair) brush that has been dipped in turpentine or odorless thinner, squeezed out or wiped clean, but still retaining enough turp to lift out paint from the canvas.

26 *Turped paper towel* A paper towel, folded in eighths, that has had about one-quarter inch of one corner dipped in turpentine or odorless thinner and then blotted on a dry paper towel pad.

27 *Turped Q-Tip* A Q-Tip that has been dipped in turpentine or odorless thinner and then blotted on a paper towel pad.

28 *Whipped cream* The consistency the paint should resemble when it has been thinned just enough to still hold "peaks," like whipped cream.

What You'll Need

- Canvas
- 1½"-width masking tape
- Odorless thinner or turp
- Fluff Stuff—soft paper towels folded into eighths, cotton balls and Q-Tips
- GEL
- To Mix: Background paint to cover area, mixed in its own separate palette. You may use any neutral background color you like, but for these demonstrations, I mixed a grey from about eight parts Titanium White to one part Ivory Black.

NOTE: *Grey backgrounds will hold overnight at room temperature and still be usable the next day. They may be held in your freezer for up to two weeks if you carefully cover the background with wax paper and store in a plastic bag. Other colors of backgrounds vary greatly in their holding time. Why risk it? Stick to grey for a while.*

Before You Begin

1. For an 8"×10" painting, mask the borders of an unstretched 10¾"×12¾" piece of canvas with masking tape, leaving a "window" that measures 8¼"×10¼" for the painting. No matter what size painting you are doing, the 1½" borders under the tape are necessary to allow enough canvas to wrap over stretcher bars for framing. Seal the tape to the canvas by smoothing the edges with your finger.

2. Squeeze out about ½" to ¾" of GEL from the tube onto your finger and smear it onto the canvas in a large S shape. With a cotton ball that has been dipped in turp and squeezed out, spread the GEL evenly over the entire area to be covered with background paint. This will "seal" the canvas under the paint and make lift-outs easier. The turpy GEL must not evaporate before you apply background paint, so proceed immediately to the background style you have selected.

The Plain Background

This is the simplest background and is the basis for all other styles. Practice on small pieces of canvas first.

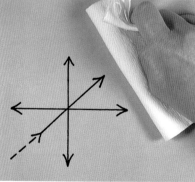

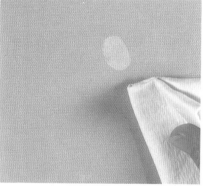

1 Fold a paper towel in eighths and dip one corner in turp about two inches up the towel. Use it as a "brush" to apply the background paint. With a glob of paint on the turpy towel, smear the entire GEL'ed canvas. The smeared paint should be loose and mobile.

2 Promptly smooth out this streaky mess with a clean, dry paper towel folded into a pad. Smooth the entire background using first horizontal and vertical strokes, and ending with diagonal strokes, using less and less pressure as you proceed.

3 Enough paint should remain on the canvas for rich color but with a "white dot" texture showing through. If paint is correctly applied and smoothed, you'll be able to lift a fingerprint with ease. Excessive smoothing with too much pressure dries out the background. Go easy!

Background Variations

HAZED BACKGROUND
Use dry paper towels and/or cotton balls to achieve a hazed effect. Repeated use of clean lift-out tools with little pressure gives the cleanest lift-out. Pat with a dry cotton ball to blend darks to lights.

CLOUDS
Experiment with dry and turped cotton balls, paper towels and Q-Tips to make clouds. Be sure to leave enough background paint under areas with animals and birds in them to create fur and feathers.

SUNRAYS
With an airplane stroke, run a dry cotton ball along a straightedge to simulate sunrays. More pressure and a clean cotton ball create the brightest rays.

ADDING PAINT
You may add darker or lighter shades of paint to backgrounds. Use a fan brush to apply and blend the paint in any shape desired.

NOTE: *Your animal is best painted on an area that's the original background color.*

The Halo

This is the most difficult background and takes practice to do well. You may want to use other background styles at first. It is essential that the halo be done quickly so the turpy paint stays loose and movable.

1 Smear a large circle of paint onto your GEL'ed background with a turpy paper towel. The paint should slide easily and glisten with turp.

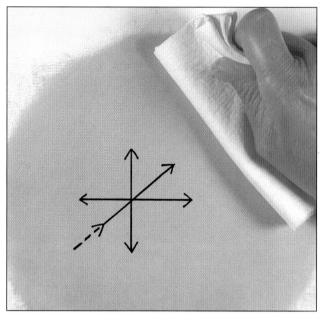

2 Smooth the paint with a dry paper towel pad held halfway back along the pad. Stroke horizontally and vertically, and finish up with "no pressure" diagonal strokes.

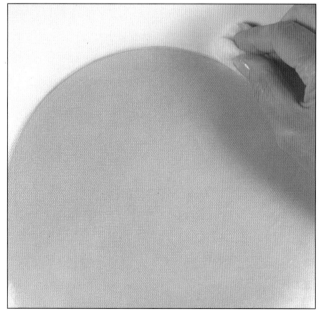

3 Thoroughly rub down all white areas surrounding the top half of the painted circle with a turpy cotton ball, reshaping your circle where necessary.

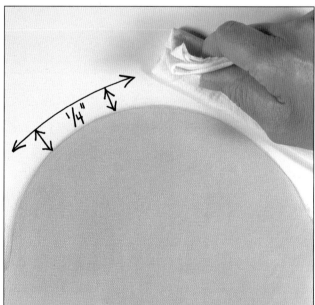

4 Wipe off all the white area with a clean paper towel pad, leaving a ¼" to ½" ring of turp around the outside of the circle.

NOTE: *It is very important to remove any residual GEL from white areas as it will discolor with age.*

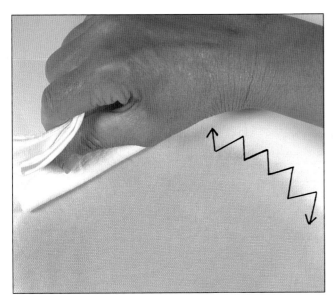

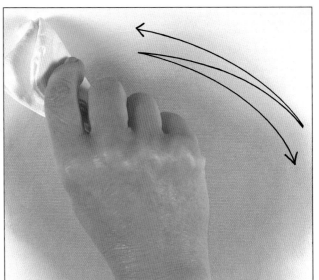

5 Using the *same side* of the pad, mush the edge of the circle using an up-and-down sunburst motion. Hold the pad about halfway back as shown, with your hand and thumb "riding" the turp ring. Again, use no pressure!

6 With the *same side* of the pad, make half-circle sweeps to further blend the circle's edge. Your thumb should still be "riding" the position of the old turp ring. The paint should still be sliding with ease.

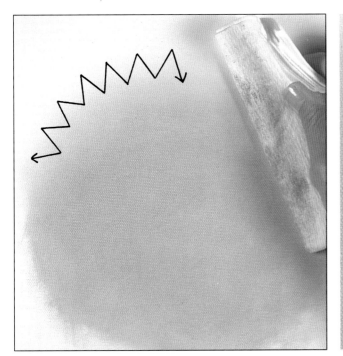

7 Finish fading your circle with a *clean side* of the paper towel pad. Use an up-and-down sunburst motion and no pressure. Turn your painting upside down and repeat Steps 3 through 7 to fade the other half of the circle.

8 Clean up any smudges where the circle touches the tape. Lift out a small area of smudge with a turped and blotted Q-Tip. With a clean, dry cotton ball, gently rub and blend the area. Repeat if necessary.

For each of the projects in this book, I have provided a full-sized stencil drawing to make it easier for you to get started. Before you begin each project, study the stencil drawing carefully and compare it to the finished painting.

You will transfer the design onto a wet background that you've already prepared with the color you wish to use.

What You'll Need
- Tracing paper or wax paper
- Pencil, stylus or ballpoint pen
- Heavy paper or card stock for a stencil
- Graphite paper (optional)
- X-Acto knife for stencil

How to Read the Stencil Drawing

In the sample stencil drawing below, the white areas show what is to be cut out for a stencil. The black lines show what is to be traced for a line drawing. The dotted lines are just painting guidelines and should not be traced. Since you are painting rather than drawing, not every detail of a design needs to be transferred to your canvas.

You may transfer your design to a prepared wet background in one of three ways: (1) with a line drawing transfer, (2) with a stencil, or (3) with a combination of the two.

To begin a line drawing transfer, trace the black lines onto tracing paper or wax paper.

To begin a stencil pattern, trace *around* the white shapes in the pattern. Where there is a black line along the edge of a white shape, trace on the black line.

Details like grass and flowers may be traced and transferred with a graphite transfer when the baby animal painting is dry.

Before you begin painting, read through the project instructions and select the design transfer option(s) you wish to use.

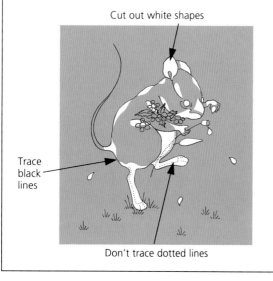

Cut out white shapes

Trace black lines

Don't trace dotted lines

Line Drawing Transfer

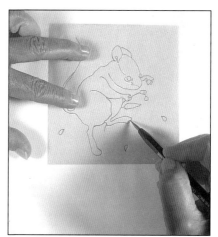

1 Place the tracing of the design on your prepared wet background. Retrace the lines with a stylus or ballpoint pen.

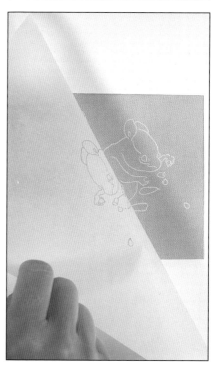

2 When you lift the tracing, a white line drawing will be on your canvas. The wet background paint from these lines is now on the back of your tracing paper.

Stencil Transfer

Stencils are particularly useful if you wish to paint a design more than once or if the design has large areas of lifted-out whites. A heavy, slick, *coated* paper (like the pages of this book) makes a good stencil.

To transfer your pattern to the stencil paper, use graphite paper under your traced drawing or simply rub a soft pencil over the lines on the back of the tracing. When retraced with a stylus or ballpoint pen, a graphite drawing will be left on your stencil paper. This will be your cutting pattern.

1 Cut the Pattern
With an X-Acto knife, cut out the "white" shapes of the pattern, being careful not to cut through small connecting points of the stencil.

2 Lift out Background Paint
Place the stencil on your prepared wet background. Lift out the background paint showing through the stencil by gently rubbing with a dry cotton ball.

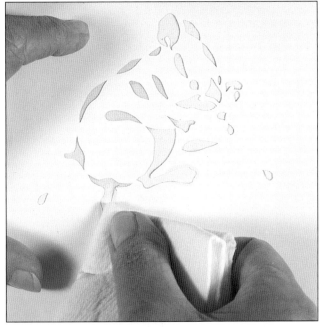

3 Use a Turped Towel
Some shapes in the stencil may need to be lifted out even whiter. Using a paper towel folded in eighths, dip only about ¼" of a folded corner of the towel in turp. Blot out this corner thoroughly on another folded towel. With *no pressure* on the towel, gently rub the shapes you want whiter.

NOTE: *A turped paper towel acts like a sponge. If it is not pressed, it will pick up a spill. If pressed, it releases liquid and makes turp bleeds behind your stencil.*

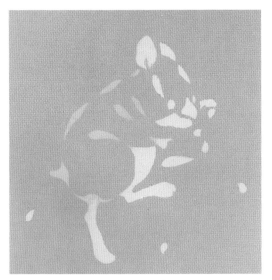

4 Remove the Stencil
When you remove your stencil, the image will appear in pale grey and white shapes. Remove stencil connection points with a Q-Tip or turp brush.

Before You Paint

Check your background for any areas that may need to be re-smoothed with a folded dry paper towel. A gentle pat-patting with the folded towel will also redistribute the wet paint.

You may use a shield to protect your wet background from smears where your hand may rest as you paint your baby animal. A piece of slick coated paper works well.

LIFTING OUT WHITES

Lifting out wet paint to expose bare canvas for the "whites" in a painting is a quick and effective method for everything from pristine snow drifts to fluffy birdlet breasts. It is also an integral part of achieving glowing, shining fur and other brilliant highlights. Three basic lifting-out principles apply:

1 *Use clean lift-out tools.* Once a tool has paint in it, it acts as a loaded brush and redeposits paint ("dirt") onto your canvas. Frequently changing sides and/or tools prevents the inclination to use a "dirty" tool.

2 *Use light pressure.* Heavy pressure only grinds the dirt into the canvas pits, making it more difficult to remove. Use evenly increasing or decreasing pressures for smooth, airbrushed-looking transitions between light and dark areas.

3 *Let the turp do the work.* The chemical has tremendous lifting capability if you give it a second or two to react with the paint before you begin lifting.

THE COTTON BALL
Dry cotton balls are used for large, soft lift-outs (such as snow drifts) and for blending turped Q-Tip highlights into the surrounding area (such as egg highlights).

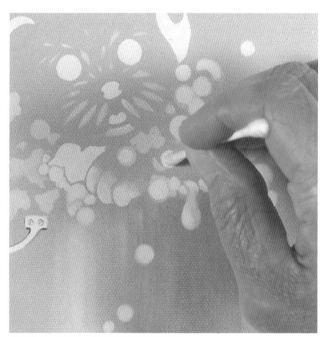

THE Q-TIP—STRAIGHT UP
Holding the Q-Tip like a pencil and perpendicular to the canvas creates round shapes like bubbles. To enlarge the shape, gradually spiral the Q-Tip in ever-larger concentric circles.

THE Q-TIP—ON THE SIDE
Grasping the Q-Tip with all four fingers along its stem is the most frequently used position. Use the side of the Q-Tip to create a variety of shapes.

Q-Tip Adjustment

Dry and turped Q-Tips sometimes need to be adjusted in size and tightness, depending on use.

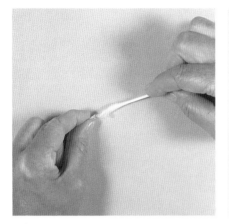  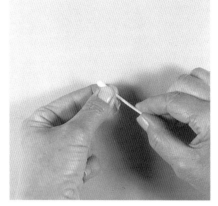

1 With a slight jiggling motion, pull out and loosen part of the cotton on the tip of the Q-Tip.

2 Wrap the loosened cotton back along the stem.

3 Push the Q-Tip up between your thumb and forefinger, twisting as you push, until it is tight. This takes a little practice, but you'll get it!

Lifting out Shapes

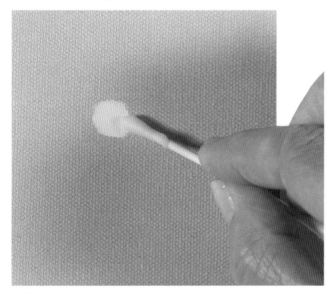 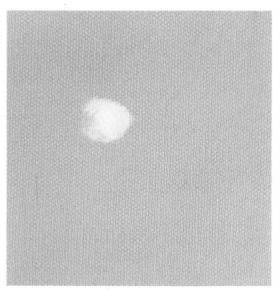

1 Using a Q-Tip on its side, start in the middle of a shape and gradually enlarge it. When using a turped Q-Tip, always begin by lightly jiggling it in place to release some turp onto the canvas.

2 Use less pressure on the Q-Tip as you approach the edge of the shape. With dry Q-Tips, this creates a haze. With turped Q-Tips, less pressure toward the edges leaves a turpy paint mush essential for further blending.

Airplaning

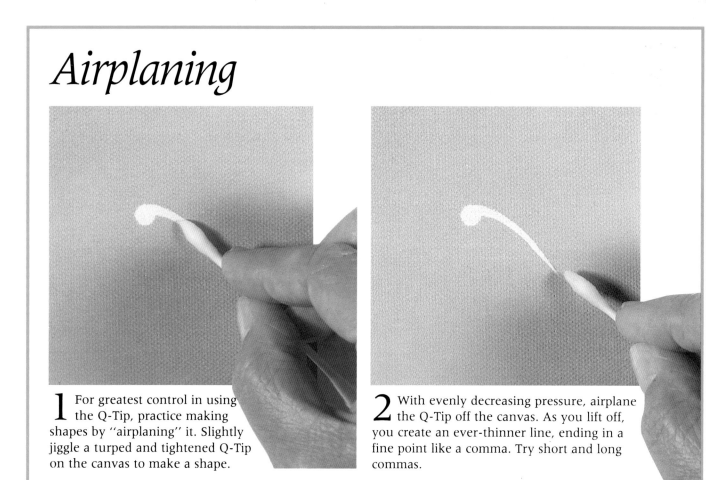

1 For greatest control in using the Q-Tip, practice making shapes by "airplaning" it. Slightly jiggle a turped and tightened Q-Tip on the canvas to make a shape.

2 With evenly decreasing pressure, airplane the Q-Tip off the canvas. As you lift off, you create an ever-thinner line, ending in a fine point like a comma. Try short and long commas.

Varying Your Lift-Out Widths

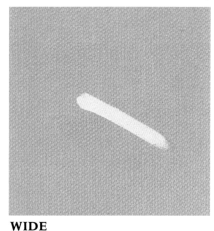 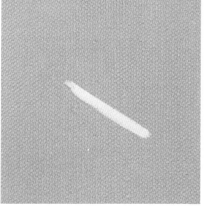 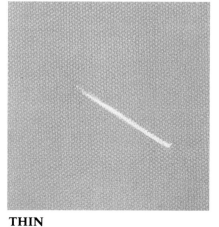

WIDE
The same Q-Tip can create many lift-out widths, depending on the pressure used. Using the side of the Q-Tip on the canvas, exert heavy pressure to create a fat lift-out.

MEDIUM
Next, try a medium width lift-out by using less pressure as you stroke.

THIN
You can get a very thin lift-out by using little to no pressure on the Q-Tip, since only a tiny area of the rounded surface will touch the canvas at one time.

Blending With a Dry Q-Tip

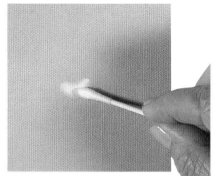

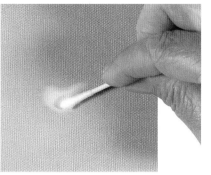

SOFTENING AN EDGE
Dry Q-Tips are used for softening edges and blending. To maintain the initial size of the lifted-out shape, gently smudge the line between the background and the white shape with a slight jiggling motion of the Q-Tip. Do not use pressure.

ENLARGING SHAPES
To enlarge shapes, use the same motion, but start in the white area. Move your dry Q-Tip gradually into the background with decreasing pressure.

REDUCING SHAPES
You can reduce the white shape easily by moving background paint into the white, gradually increasing pressure as you approach the center. The size and brightness of your shape are always up to you!

Lifting With a Turp Brush

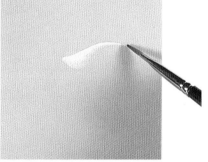

THE TURP BRUSH
The turp brush is always a *bright* brush, no matter what size. It must be used on the back corner of the chisel edge to be an effective lift-out tool.

AIRPLANING
After pressing and jiggling the brush slightly to release some turp onto the canvas, lightly sweep the brush in an airplaning stroke. The top line of your shape will be cleanly lifted, while the bottom will remain hazy.

SCOOTING THE PAINT AHEAD
Occasionally you'll want to use the turp brush with its chisel flat on the canvas. This creates very fine lines or enlarges shapes by scooting the paint ahead of the brush.

HOW TO PAINT FUR

Painting realistic-looking fur can be faster and easier than you think! As you follow these techniques for creating fur, remember the most important element is your eye. If the fur doesn't *look* right, repeat or alter the process until it does.

BEFORE YOU PAINT
On a palette put out *small* amounts of the oil colors you'll be using and a small mound of GEL. Leave enough room next to each dollop of color to thin the color as you need it. Here, I'm thinning the red paint.

The Paint Pattern

The "paint pattern" is the secret to creating realistic-looking fur with the depth and richness of layered colors. And the best thing is, you don't have to *mix* all your fur colors on your palette beforehand!

Compare the paint pattern (below right) to the finished painting (below left). Try to make sense of this "camouflage paint suit" by finding which areas of the paint pattern relate to which areas on the finished animal. Take special note of the deep shadow areas.

Translate which strokes must be accurately painted so as to maintain the animal's shape (such as the nose); which strokes are scrumbled in messily to provide fur color (on his back); and which are "negative" strokes

PALETTE

that serve to define another shape (as around the ear). With practice, you will be able to develop your own paint patterns from animal photos—the first step to painting your own pet!

FINISHED PAINTING

PAINT PATTERN

Maintain shapes accurately

Define negative shapes

Scrumble color loosely

How to Build the Paint Pattern

1 Paint Darks and Shadow Areas
First, paint any pink areas (such as inside the ear) and shade them with a dry and/or turped Q-Tip. Then, heavily load a bright brush with "whipped cream" paint in your darkest fur color. The paint should flow off the brush and float on top of the background paint. Paint dark shadow areas and dark-colored fur areas.

2 Scrumble in Darks
As the brush unloads its dark paint, move to areas on the bunny that need less dark paint. Scrumble in large, loose strokes that allow the background grey color to show through like "dots."

3 Scrumble in Lighter Colors
Scrumble in lighter colors, leaving some background showing. Large S-shaped strokes, of varying depth of paint, will brush out into the most realistic-looking fur.

4 Float on Remaining Colors
Remaining colors may be scrumbled over previous colors, floating the paint on top as much as possible. Looser paint and a heavily loaded brush will help.

Your paint pattern is now ready to be brushed into a whole range of shades of fur without your having to mix each shade on your palette!

Before You Brush the Fur . . .

Study fur. Grab a patient pet and really look at the fur! Is it long or short, sleek or fluffy, coarse or fine, straight or curly? Most fur is straight and does not curve much along the length of the hair unless it is very long. Many animals—like cats, foxes and squirrels—have several lengths of fur, from very short on the face to very long on the tail.

As you are painting, think of the length of each hair on the real animal and then adjust the length proportionately on your animal. Pretend you are grooming a real animal as you brush the painted fur.

In this diagram, the arrows indicate the direction of fur growth. Most fur grows from the tip of the nose, over the head and back, down the tummy, and out toward the extremities (ears, paws and tail).

The greater the angle, the fluffier the animal.

The angle of the fur to the skin determines how sleek or fluffy an animal is. The smaller the angle, the sleeker the animal.

As you layer the fur on your painting, wrap it around and over the curves of the animal's body for a three-dimensional effect. It may help to think of this as the "mummy bunny" effect.

Remember: Successful fur also depends on accurate *observation* of the rotation and angle of each hair, since perspective will sometimes make it appear to be going in the wrong direction.

Sometimes you see only the tip of the hair as it points directly toward your eye. Perspective makes the hair appear progressively longer as it tilts away from your eye.

Brushing Fur With a Bristle Brush

Raking through the paint pattern with a stiff bristle round brush and a light pressure creates many hair lines at once. The more perpendicular to the canvas you hold the brush, the more hair lines will be made.

Always dip the brush in turp or thinner, blot it out, and then moisten it in GEL before brushing. Repeatedly wipe out, re-turp, and re-GEL your brush as you work.

These strokes shown below may be used in any combination to quickly create realistic-looking fur.

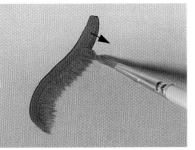

Dragging out is the most common stroke. Always airplane the brush for fine-pointed fur tips.

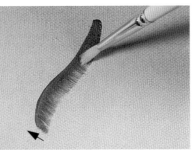

Dragging in with a clean brush thins out heavy fur tips. Airplane in from the tips to the roots of the fur, wiping out the brush after each stroke.

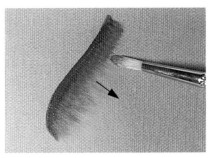

Dragging in with a dirty brush places paint ("dirt") at an exact point. Use this stroke for controlled short fur edges to prevent the animal from "growing."

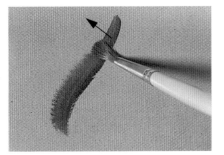

Splatting (stippling) pushes the paint ahead of the bristles. Use this stroke for short edge fur or for moving paint that won't slide as it should.

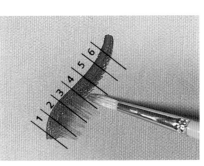

Overlapping of strokes should be kept to a minimum. Excessive overlapping creates a velveteen look at best and a mush at worst.

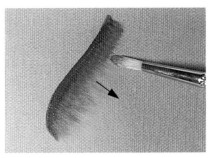

Extending thin fur, as on tails, is done by dragging out a tiny bit of paint from an already-brushed edge. Use no overlap and plenty of GEL for the best look.

LET'S PRACTICE BRUSHING A FURRY BALL

1 Paint a ball on a prepared wet background. With a dragging-out stroke, brush a layer of fur around the edge. Make sure that the angles of each stroke are rotating evenly "around the clock."

2 Add successive layers by spiraling them toward the center. Overlap each fur layer's tips over the previous layer's roots. Perspective will make each layer appear shorter as it nears the center.

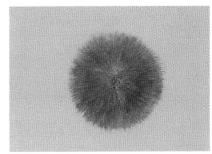

3 Stipple the center where only the tips of the fur are visible. Scan your furry ball to make sure it looks groomed. Lightly re-brush any scruffy edges and check for even rotation of angles in the fur.

The Rough Brush

The rough (or first) brush should be neat and tidy but not overworked. Go easy, and use a light touch, with little or no overlapping. Wipe out, re-turp and re-GEL your brush often to prevent traveling of color.

1 Study this fur diagram for fur direction and decide how long or short and how sleek or fuzzy you want your bunny's fur to be.

2 Begin by brushing the fur farthest away from view, along the edges of the animal.

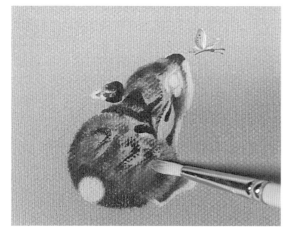

3 Brush in an underneath layer of fur. Airplane the tips over any previous layer's roots.

4 Continue to wrap layers of fur over the animal in one area at a time, like fringe on a flapper dress.

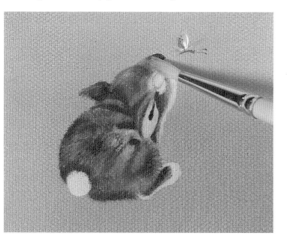

5 The fur tips should now extend over the roots and all angles should rotate correctly.

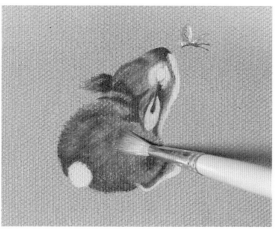

6 For areas where you look straight down the fur and see only the tips of each hair, use a light stipple stroke. (See Step 3 on the previous page.)

Your animal now looks furry, but it needs a good hair conditioner to bring out its shine!

Glow and Re-Brush

"Glowing" simulates the reflection of light on the fur and results in a fantastic three-dimensional, realistic effect. Fur comes to life when you glow it. This is also the grooming stage of brushing fur. As you glow, check surrounding fur for any improvements you can make.

Before You Glow . . .
Compare the glow pattern (below right) to the finished bunny painting (below left). Plan to glow the large, easy areas first. Do only one or two glow areas at a time, as the turp or thinner must not evaporate before the glow is re-brushed.

NOTE: *Some projects in this book use white paint in place of exposed canvas to create a glow. The basic principles remain the same.*

FINISHED PAINTING

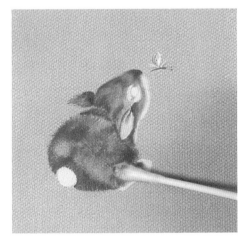

GLOW PATTERN

Dry-Glowing Techniques

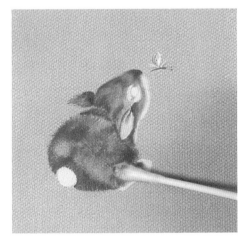

1 Dry Q-Tip glowing is used for less highlighted glows, or where the fur needs to be lighter in color. Lift the area with a clean, dry Q-Tip.

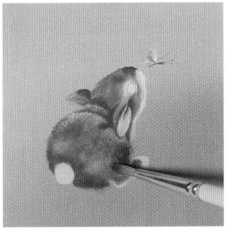

2 Then re-brush with added GEL in your bristle brush, repeating until you have achieved the desired color level.

Turped Q-Tip Glowing Techniques

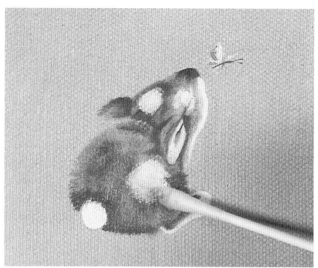

1 Turped Q-Tip glowing is used for bright highlights. Turped Q-Tips should always be blotted before using. Lift paint from the area to be glowed by slightly jiggling the Q-Tip to release a bit of turp onto the area. Enlarge the shape, using no pressure. The area should be larger than the final highlight and should have a ''turpy-painty'' ring around it.

2 Now re-brush the outer edges of the glow and gradually move through the turpy ring. Leave a white pinpoint area by never letting the brush touch the center. Wipe out and re-GEL your brush often so as not to travel too much color. The GEL also holds the shape of the individual hair marks. Repeat as needed if your glow disappears or is the wrong shape. This is no-fail painting!

Turp-Brush Glowing Techniques

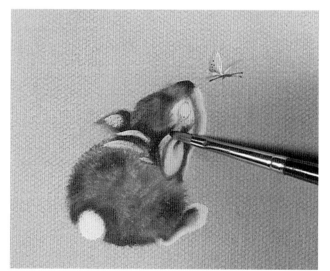

1 Turp-brush glowing is used for highlights too tiny for a Q-Tip. Lift out the glow area with a bright sable brush that has been dipped in turp or thinner and squeezed or wiped out. Always stroke with the brush on the back corner of the chisel. Carefully re-brush with GEL—these tiny glows can disappear as quickly as you make them.

2 Individual shiny hairs are made with a turp brush. An airplane motion creates fine hair tips with no residual turpy ring around them. If necessary, blend the base of the hairs by re-brushing with your bristle brush. Be selective in the number and placement of shiny hairs. It's so much fun to do, you may have a porcupine before you know it!

FINISHING TRICKS

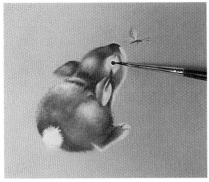

Sharp, crisp edges on eyes, ribbons and other accessories are created by first painting the middle of the shape and then stretching the paint toward the edges. Keep in mind that you're painting—not drawing and coloring.

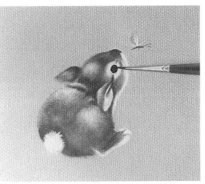

Small, hard shapes, like eyes, are best done with loose paint. Let the paint flow off a heavily loaded brush and then move the paint in an ever-larger circle, with the hairs of the brush touching only the paint—not the canvas. Gradually sneak up on the final shape by stirring your puddle.

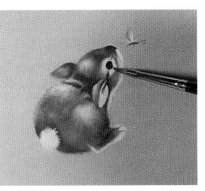

Clean-up is easy with a turp-brush "eraser." The turp brush sharpens painted edges, enlarges white shapes, and performs myriad other tasks. Let it work for you!

Pinpoint highlights are best done with a heavily loaded brush. Let the paint flow off the brush. If the hairs of the brush never touch the underlying paint, a sparkling highlight will float on the surface.

Pinpoint darks help define the animal's shape. Always use less than you think, as only a touch of dark blended into the deepest shadows goes a long way. This may be done when the fur is dry if you add some GEL to the dark paint and "glaze" the area.

Fine lines, like grasses, pine tree needles and antennae, are best done with a fully loaded brush, no pressure, and an airplane stroke. Always test the stroke on junk canvas. Holding your breath sometimes helps with detail work, too!

And Finally . . .

- *Cobalt drier* is usually not appropriate for use in fur but can be helpful to accelerate the drying time of finish work. Just a drop or two mixed in the paint will result in an overnight drying time.
- *Your signature* is a vital part of the composition. The style of your signature and its placement and color can either enhance or detract from your painting. It's the last but always important detail!

- *Picture varnish* may be applied after the painting is thoroughly dry. Two or three light coats of Damar gloss or other good picture varnish will make areas of "sunken" color reappear. The varnish also seals the surface from dirt and other damage.

harris

1

HOW TO PAINT
A Little Mouse

"He Loves Me!"

This perky little mouse was inspired by a darling woodland mouse who lived under my studio steps. Gertrude has appeared in many of my paintings and is still one of my favorite subjects. She always makes me smile!

What You'll Need

- Oil paints—*GEL, Titanium White, Ivory Black, Raw Umber, Cadmium Yellow Light, Red, Sap Green, Burnt Sienna*
- Mix these colors—*background grey, fawn, pink, deep yellow-orange, grass green*
- Canvas—*with prepared background*
- Brushes—*small bristle round, tiny sable round, small sable bright, medium sable bright*
- X-Acto knife
- Q-Tips, cotton balls, soft paper towels
- Odorless thinner

Before You Begin

1. Using the stencil drawing on the previous page, cut a stencil or trace a line drawing of the image.
2. Transfer the image to your prepared wet background.

NOTE: *The tail, grass, and flower stems are easiest if transferred with a graphite transfer after the painting is dry, and then painted. Do not transfer the bouquet, as it will also be painted later.*

1 Lift out Whites

With a turped paper towel and stencil, a turped Q-Tip or a turp brush, lift out the wet grey background paint from the ears, eyes, tummy area, muzzle, feet, tossed petals and flower. Even if you use a stencil, you may need to perfect some of these areas with a turp-brush clean-up. If you use a line drawing transfer, you may wish to lift out some highlight areas on the head and hip. Define the tummy by painting in some grey and softening the paint with a dry Q-Tip.

2 *Add Pink to the Ear*

With a small brush, put some pink color in the ear. There's no need to be too precise.

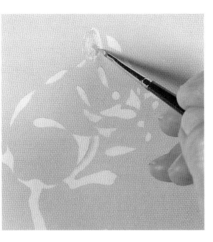

3 *Glow the Ear*

Using a dry Q-Tip, gently rub the ear pink until it's the shape and shade you wish. Rub with a clean, dry Q-Tip when you want the pink to be lighter.

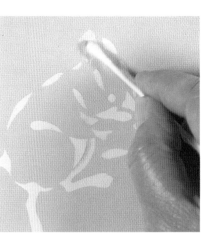

4 *Paint Shadows and Darks*

Paint the shadows and dark Raw Umber areas first, using a small bright brush. Your paint should be of whipped-cream consistency and should easily flow off the heavily loaded brush. As the brush unloads, move to the more sketchy areas of the paint pattern. In these places you want the paint to skip and leave "grey dots" showing through.

Remember to use more precise strokes in areas that define another shape (like under the cheek), and very squiggly strokes in areas where you are simply providing color for the fur.

5 *Scrumble in Color*

The secret to scrumbling in the fawn color is to use large S shapes, and not to use too much paint. Notice how much grey background still shows through? You can always add more color if you need it. Just stay loose and squiggle—even over some of the brown. Your mouse should now look like a mess with no tail!

6 *The Fur Pattern*

Take a minute to relate this fur diagram to the fur brush marks in the finished painting on page 30, and then in the photo of the rough brush (below).

See how the fur grows from the tip of the nose out to the paws and tail tip? If you imagine it on your own body, it will help you "feel" the fur as it grows over and around the body. Before you begin brushing out the fur, decide how long, short, sleek or fuzzy this fur is.

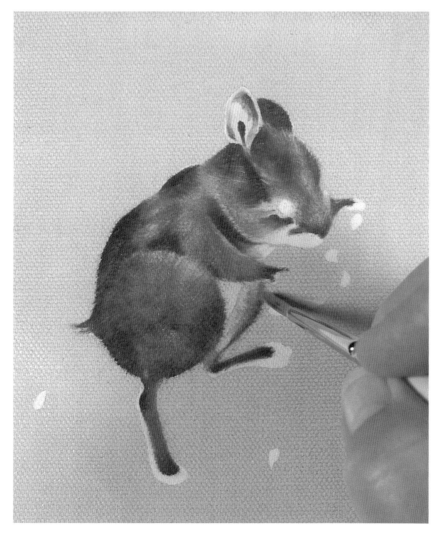

7 *Rough-Brush the Fur*

Dip your bristle brush in turp, blot it, and then moisten it in a small amount of GEL before you brush. Begin brushing in a few easy places, like the back's edge, paying special attention to the angle of the fur. Wipe out your brush frequently and re-GEL it.

After the major edges have been brushed, begin to layer the fur on a large area like the head or hip. Start with underneath layers, layering new hair tips over the previous layer's roots.

When you reach some round parts very close to you, just the tips of each hair will be visible. Stipple these areas.

Now your mouse is looking more realistic but is still having a "bad hair day."

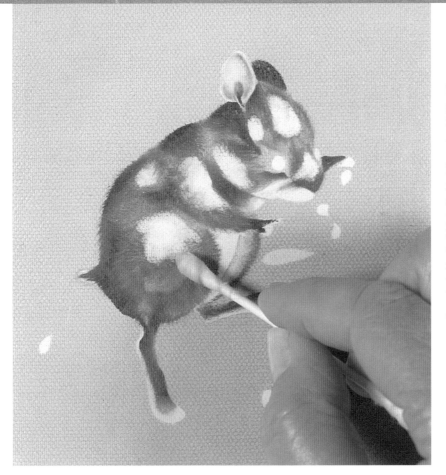

8 *Glow Some Areas*

Soften and blend the dark brown in the pink ear by rubbing gently with a dry Q-Tip. Always using a clean, dry Q-Tip, soften other areas of the ear, toes and muzzle.

Using a turped Q-Tip that has been blotted, gently remove paint from areas to be highlighted. A slight jiggling motion and a light pressure will ensure a turpy paint ring is left around a bright white center area. These rings produce a range of midtone fur colors when they're brushed. Glow and re-brush just one or two highlights at a time.

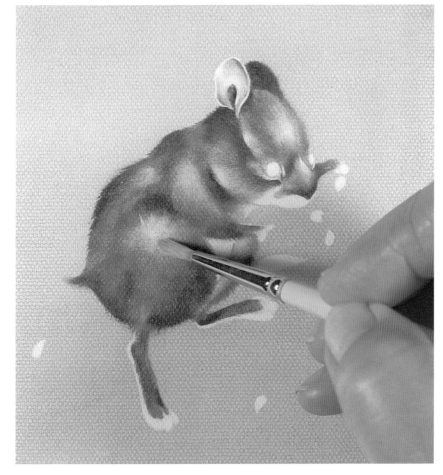

9 *Re-Brush and Groom*

After moistening your cleaned bristle brush with GEL, re-brush your glowed areas. Keep the brush clean and re-GEL'ed as you approach the white center. Retain bright pinpoint centers by never letting the brush touch them. You may have to glow and re-brush the same area several times to achieve the effect you want.

Some areas may need a bit more color or even some Burnt Sienna added for warmth. Mix a small amount of paint into some GEL and apply it directly with the bristle brush, brushing and blending as you go.

Check your mouse thoroughly, making sure all the fur looks pretty and groomed. With a light touch, you can re-brush any messy areas. Continue reworking until you are satisfied, because at this stage, almost anything can be fixed!

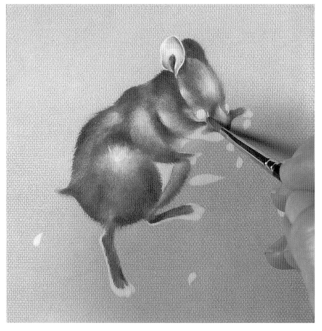

10 *Enhance and Clean Up*
With a turp brush, enhance and clean up the ear, muzzle, eye fur, tummy and toes.

At this point it is possible to let the painting dry and finish it later. If you are stopping, skip ahead and add the mouse's whiskers.

11 *Puddle in the Eyes*
With a full load of whipped-cream-consistency black on a tiny round brush, let a droplet of paint flow from the brush onto the middle of the eye. Gently stir this puddle until it's the correct size and shape. This method makes very crisp, accurate edges.

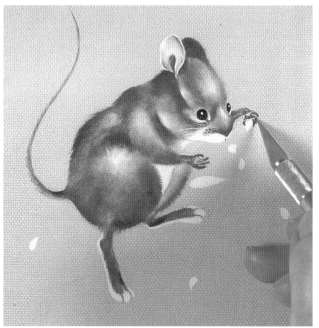

12 *Add White to Highlight*
Load a tiny round brush with whipped-cream-consistency white paint. Gently float a tiny droplet on the black for the eye highlight. Using white paint, perk up any areas you may want brighter—around the eye, feet, ear highlights, or the tossed petals. Add toe lines with a tiny brush.

13 *Add Whiskers and Tail*
Finish your mouse with some whisker dots. Paint the tail using a fawn and GEL mixture, then very gently glow and brush it. Paint the hands, blending them into the wrist fur. Glowing the fingers with a small bright turp brush is a nice touch. Scratch out whiskers with an X-Acto knife.

Painting the Flowers

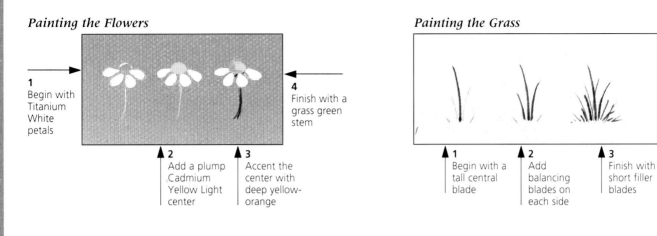

1
Begin with Titanium White petals

2
Add a plump Cadmium Yellow Light center

3
Accent the center with deep yellow-orange

4
Finish with a grass green stem

Painting the Grass

1
Begin with a tall central blade

2
Add balancing blades on each side

3
Finish with short filler blades

14 Final Touches

After your painting is dry, paint in some flowers and grass. It's easy to be creative now, since mistakes are easily removed with turped Q-Tips or a turp brush.

You may even want to change the flowers to holly leaves with red berries, add a few snowflakes, and call your painting "Fa-la-la-la-lah."

Whatever you decide, be sure to sign your painting in a size, place and color that will complement your little mouse! Your signature is an integral part of your painting. Be proud of it—everyone wants to know the artist!

harris

2

HOW TO PAINT

Baby Birds

"Grounded!"

Baby birds, like many baby animals, seem to be a bit suspended in time—no future, no consequences.
I frequently draw upon this endearing quality when I'm depicting a cute scenario.
I created these birdlets after watching three baby wrens
attempt their first flight on my patio.

What You'll Need

- Oil paints—*GEL, Titanium White, Ivory Black, Raw Umber, Burnt Sienna, Cadmium Yellow Light, Sap Green, Red*
- Mix these colors—*background grey, pink, grass green*
- Canvas—*with prepared background*
- Brushes—*small bristle round, tiny sable round, small sable bright, medium sable bright*
- Q-Tips, cotton balls, soft paper towels
- Odorless thinner

Before You Begin

1. Using the stencil drawing on the previous page, cut a stencil or trace a line drawing of the image.
2. Transfer the image to your prepared wet background.

NOTE: *Grass, feet and pine needles may be graphite-transferred to the painting after it has dried, and painted last.*

1 Lift out Whites and Feathers

With a turped paper towel and stencil or a turp brush, lift out the wet grey background paint from the ladybug and the birdlets' eyes and beaks. With a turp brush, lift out the background grey from the wings and breast of the top bird. Blend and make feather streaks with a bristle brush that has been moistened in turp. Repeat this process on the lowest bird.

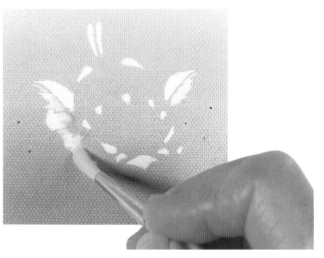

2 Lift out Feathers

With a turped Q-Tip, lift out clumps of feathers from the middle bird's breast. Leave enough grey to create shadows when it is brushed, or the birdlet's breast won't appear to be soft and fluffy. Check the diagram on page 42 for feather direction.

3 Blend and Brush Feathers

Using a bristle brush moistened with turp, gently blend the clumps, making some streak marks to indicate down and feathers. To avoid leaving a grey ring on the outer edge, brush back in toward the breast.

4 Paint Shadows and Darks

Heavily load your small bright brush with Raw Umber that you have thinned to whipped-cream consistency. Paint the top birdlet's tail feathers first. Place the brush at the top of each tail mark, pressing slightly. As you stroke down toward the body, evenly and gradually decrease the pressure. This should leave a perfectly shaped and tapered "feather."

Continue the paint pattern of darks and shadows on the birds' bodies and heads, making the sketchy strokes as the brush unloads.

5 Scrumble Burnt Sienna

Scrumble in some Burnt Sienna on the birdlets' cheeks. At this time, compare the intensity of your paint pattern to these photos. You will need a sufficient amount of paint in each area to stretch through the grey areas when you begin brushing out the birdlets' downy feathers. You can add or remove paint later, but it is always prettiest if the levels are correct to begin with.

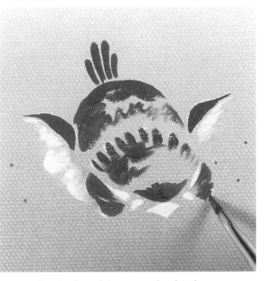

6 Brush the Top Bird

Compare this feather diagram for the top bird to the photo at right. Notice the direction and angles of the feathers as they go from the beak, over the back, and out to the tips of the wings.

After brushing the top edges of each shape with the bristle brush, begin to layer the feathers, overlapping the tips over the base of the previous layer. Wipe out and re-GEL your brush often as you work. You need enough GEL to break and move the dark paint pattern.

7 Brush the Middle Bird

Check this middle bird feather diagram for the feather angles and direction before you brush. Feathers that brush out too dark may be lifted with a dry Q-Tip and re-brushed with GEL.

The head should look as if the birdlet has a crew cut. Extend these feathers using the bristle brush on its back edge, with only a few bristles touching the canvas. Use paint from only the tips of the crew cut feathers. If you grab too much paint, you will simply extend the crew cut, rather than create the illusion of wind ruffling the feathers.

8 ***Groom and Enhance the Top Bird***
With a small turp brush, clean out the areas around the eyes of the top bird. Using a tiny round brush, paint in a squiggly beak. Indicate the scrunched-up closed eyes with "half-moon" eyelashes. Finish the beak with a turp glow.

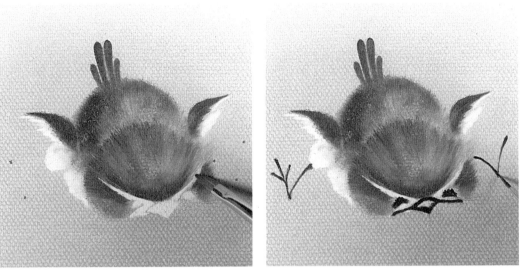

   Make perfect feet by heavily loading a tiny round brush with loose black paint. Starting with a gentle press on the toes, gradually release pressure on the brush as you stroke toward the base. The feet may be done when the painting is dry.

9 ***Groom and Enhance the Middle Bird***
Clean the eye areas of the middle bird with a turp brush. Puddle in the eyes with a tiny round brush, stirring and stretching the puddle until it's the correct size and shape.
   Paint the beak with a

sheer coat of rather sticky yellow, using a small bright brush. Wipe out the brush (no turp) and add a coat of sticky Burnt Sienna. Wipe out the brush (no turp) and blend the yellow into the Burnt Sienna. Follow the steps shown below, using soupy pink and white floated on the other colors. Finally, highlight the eyes and paint the feet.

Painting the Middle Bird's Beak

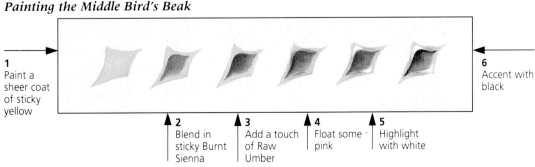

1 Paint a sheer coat of sticky yellow

2 Blend in sticky Burnt Sienna

3 Add a touch of Raw Umber

4 Float some pink

5 Highlight with white

6 Accent with black

10 ***The Lower Bird: Paint the Darks***
Paint the tail of the lower bird using Raw Umber and a small bright brush. Finish the Raw Umber paint pattern, leaving plenty of grey behind the head. The expression will be cuter if you keep the Raw Umber very low and close over the eyes and beak. Scrumble in Burnt Sienna for added color and interest.

11 ***Brush the Lower Bird***
Compare the feather diagram (above) to the photo (at right). Moisten your bristle brush with GEL and brush the major edge areas of the image. Starting at the back and working forward, make layers of short feathers.

12 ***Paint the Eyes and Beak***
Clear the eye and beak area with a small turp brush. Puddle in the eyes with a tiny round brush, stirring and stretching the puddle to the correct shape and size. Paint and glow the beak, turning down the corners of the "mouth."

Place the eye highlights so that the birdlet *looks* at the ladybug. If you need to change the placement of the highlight, just blot it out gently with a dry Q-Tip and try again. If at first you don't succeed. . . .

13 *Paint the Pine Branch*
Paint the tree branch using a small bright brush double-loaded with a bit of Raw Umber and a bit of GEL. This combination tends to automatically shade itself if stroked on with one wavy line at a time. Notice how the chisel edge of the small bright brush makes clean small branches, too. It's a very versatile brush.

Painting the Ladybug
Begin the ladybug with a small red puddle. Stir and stretch the paint to the correct size and shape. For crisp black accents, use a tiny round brush loaded with a bead of loose paint on the tip. Using no pressure and keeping the brush a hair above the canvas, let the paint flow off the brush and float on the surface. A slight press of the brush will enlarge the line or area.

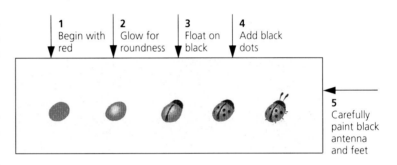

1 Begin with red

2 Glow for roundness

3 Float on black

4 Add black dots

5 Carefully paint black antenna and feet

14 *Final Touches*
Add pine needles using loose paint and a tiny round brush. Be sure to airplane off each stroke to achieve beautiful pointed tips. You may wish to wait until your painting is dry to do this delicate work.

Finish your scene with some soft, springy clumps of grass. Now your birdlets will have a safe landing and a happy ending!

HOW TO PAINT

A Fawn and a Bunny

"Friends for Life"

Most animal artists stand in awe of nature's original, especially when we paint a fawn.
It seems there's no way to make it cuter or more beautiful than it is in reality, but we keep trying.
All of us who love animals have a bit of Bambi in us, it seems.

What You'll Need

- Oil paints—*GEL, Titanium White, Ivory Black, Raw Umber, Cadmium Yellow Light, Burnt Sienna, Red, Sap Green*
- Mix these colors—*background grey, fawn, pink, deep yellow-orange, grass green*
- Canvas—*with prepared background*
- Brushes—*small bristle round, tiny sable round, small sable bright, medium sable bright*
- X-Acto knife
- Q-Tips, cotton balls, soft paper towels
- Odorless thinner

Before You Begin

1. Using the stencil drawing on the previous page, cut a stencil or trace a line drawing of the image.
2. Transfer the image to your prepared wet background.

NOTE: *If you use a stencil, remove the fawn's breast with a dry cotton ball, lifting only enough grey to allow you to see the shape. Grass may be graphite-transferred after the painting is dry.*

1 Lift out Whites

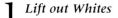

Lift out the wet grey background paint from the inside-ear fur, eyes, the fur surrounding the eyes, muzzles, tails, bunny paws, and butterfly. Use a turped Q-Tip, a turp brush, or a stencil with a turped paper towel. If you use a stencil, check for areas you must remove by hand.

With a turped Q-Tip, lift out some of the grey in the fawn's breast. Moisten your bristle brush in turp and lightly brush around these highlights in the direction the fur grows. Try to avoid making grey "hairs" in the brightest white areas. You may also want to add some grey paint for shadows and blend it with the bristle brush.

2 *Paint Shadows and Darks*

Before you paint, add pink to the insides of the ears and on the muzzles, using a brush or pink paint on a dry Q-Tip. With a clean, dry Q-Tip, gently lighten and blend the pinks.

Now, compare the dark paint pattern shown in this photo to the finished painting on page 46. Notice which brown shapes are important shadows that define a lighter shape (like under the chin and behind the hip), and which brown shapes only serve to provide fur color.

Heavily load a small bright brush with Raw Umber you have thinned to whipped-cream consistency. Begin to paint the darkest areas first, like under the chin. As the brush unloads, move to areas where you want the paint to skip and be lighter when brushed into fur. Paint the ear rim fur with an unloaded brush in short strokes in the direction the fur grows.

3 *Scrumble in Color*

Lightly scrumble in fawn color throughout the image. Be sure to use large, squiggly shapes and to leave plenty of grey background paint showing. By doing this, you will automatically achieve an incredible range of colors and values when you brush the fur with the bristle brush.

With a little experience, you'll be able to decipher where to be precise in painting these patterns and where to get wild; but it will always look this weird or worse at this stage.

4 *The Fur Pattern*

Before you begin the rough brush, compare the fur diagram to the finished painting and to the photo of the rough brush. Be sure you understand how the fur grows down the fawn's legs, even as they bend.

Because the bunny is very cute, and also very fluffy on his backside in this design, the fur directions are depicted as if his bottom were a large powder puff. A more realistic approach would direct the fur downward toward the tail.

5 *Rough-Brush the Fur*

Dip your dry bristle brush in turp and then wipe it out. This prepares brushes for the paint. Moisten the bristle brush with GEL and brush the edges of the ears and head. Remind yourself as you brush that fawns have very short fur.

After layering the fur on the ears and head, move to the top edge of the back. As you brush down the back to the tail, be aware of the angle of the fur as it pops off the edge of the image. Be sure to wipe out your brush and re-GEL often.

Proceed by brushing the edge fur and filling in the layers in one large area of the body at a time. Remember to wrap the layers around the forms, beginning with the underneath layers. Pay particular attention to the fawn's hip, making sure you have rotated your brush marks correctly as the fur pops up and over the muscle.

6 Glow Some Areas

Some areas of your fawn may need to be glowed or lightened with a dry Q-Tip. Places to dry-glow and re-brush with GEL might be the shoulder, back, hip, and brown fur next to the breast. The dry Q-Tip is also a good tool to blend and soften muzzles, bunny paws and inner ears.

For bright highlights, remove paint with a turped Q-Tip or a turp brush. To ensure that the turpy residue doesn't evaporate, glow and re-brush only one or two highlights at a time.

7 Re-Brush and Groom

Frequently wipe clean and re-GEL your bristle brush as you re-brush glowed areas. Without enough GEL, the fur marks disintegrate as quickly as you brush them.

Choose which highlights you wish to retain with bright pinpoint white centers and which ones you wish to brush through the centers for softer, hazier highlights. Too many bright highlights will polka-dot your fawn and play havoc with the flow of your composition.

For richness, you may want to directly add some color with the bristle brush. It helps your control to add GEL to the paint, particularly when you're adding Burnt Sienna. In other places, you may wish to accent forms with some pinpoint darks. Paint these over the fur and then gently re-brush.

8 Enhance the Details

To make the fawn's hoof appear shiny and hard, glow it with a turp brush. Besides being a good clean-up tool, a small turp brush can add individual hairs to the fur inside the ear and help fuzz the bunny's tail. If your whites have become stained, you may add some white paint, carefully blending it into its surrounding area.

Painting the Fawn's Eye and Nose

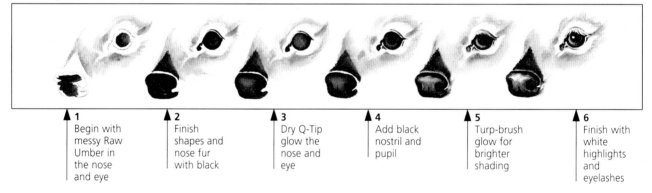

1 Begin with messy Raw Umber in the nose and eye

2 Finish shapes and nose fur with black

3 Dry Q-Tip glow the nose and eye

4 Add black nostril and pupil

5 Turp-brush glow for brighter shading

6 Finish with white highlights and eyelashes

9 Finish the Bunny

Finish your bunny by puddling in a small black eye. Gently float a droplet of white paint on the black for the highlight. Add the whisker dots and scratch out the whiskers with an X-Acto knife.

10 Lift out the Fawn's Spots

Lift out spots with a small turp brush. (The turp brush is best used on its back corner.) Vary the size and shape of the spots for a realistic look. Very lightly brush some or all of the spots with a bristle brush, dulling some to look more shadowed.

Painting the Butterfly

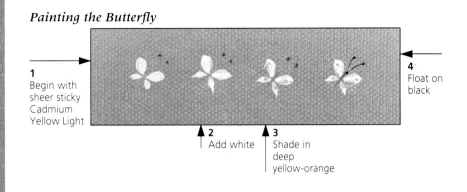

1
Begin with
sheer sticky
Cadmium
Yellow Light

2
Add white

3
Shade in
deep
yellow-orange

4
Float on
black

11 *Final Touches*
The butterfly and grasses are easiest if painted after your painting has dried. A small bright brush is a good choice for some of the larger blades of grass. Your grass will have sharp, precise tips if you always airplane the brush down onto and up off the canvas.

Attention to these final touches, along with a good, well-placed signature, are essential to the success of your painting. The love must go into the canvas before the love can come out!

4

HOW TO PAINT
A Long-Haired Pup

"Rub-a-dub Pup"

This painting is particularly fun to do! The lifted-out whites of the bubble bath and fur
make for instant gratification, as shading is created almost as if by magic.
Besides all that, I can't resist the bewildered expression—can you?

What You'll Need
- Oil paints—*GEL, Titanium White, Ivory Black, Raw Umber, Cadmium Yellow Light, Red, Burnt Sienna, Prussian Blue*
- Mix these colors—*background grey, dark grey, pink*
- Canvas—*with prepared background*
- Brushes—*small bristle round, tiny sable round, small sable bright, medium sable bright*
- X-Acto knife
- Q-Tips, cotton balls, soft paper towels
- Odorless thinner

Before You Begin
1. Using the stencil drawing on the previous page, cut a stencil or trace a line drawing of the image.
2. Transfer the image to your prepared wet background.

NOTE: *Cut or trace only as many bubbles as you feel you'll need to paint the image. If you use a stencil, remove the bubbles with a cotton ball, lifting only enough grey to see the shapes.*

1 Lift out Whites
Lift out the wet grey background paint from the eyes, nose, ear tips, tongue, paw, duck and bucket handle. Use a turped Q-Tip, a turp brush, or a stencil and turped paper towel. If you use a line drawing transfer, you may wish to lift some whites in the muzzle.

NOTE: *As long as there is no paint on the puppy, you may stop work at any time and hold your work in the freezer. To do this, carefully seal the painting in plastic wrap and store in your freezer for up to two weeks. This will allow you to proceed at your leisure.*

2 Shape the Bucket

With a clean, dry cotton ball, lift out some large, streaky highlights in the center of the bucket. Always use a clean side of the cotton ball, rather than pressure, for the greatest amount of lift-out.

Hold a stiff paper straightedge lined up on the side of the bucket. With a dry cotton ball or a brush, put dark grey paint on the sides of the bucket. Blend it gently with a clean, dry cotton ball. Be careful not to extend the shading too far down in the painting. If it becomes too dark, gently remove some paint with a clean cotton ball.

3 Paint the Bucket Handle

Using a turp brush, clean out and shape the bucket handle. Paint in the dark grey shadows and bolts with a tiny round brush.

4 Lift out the Bubbles
Bubbles are best lifted out using the tip, rather than the side, of the Q-Tip. Hold a turped Q-Tip perpendicular to the canvas and move it in tiny circles. This will produce almost perfect round bubbles. Do all the larger bubbles, leaving lots of grey area for shading later. Just like real suds, these are easy to make and hard to get rid of. You can always add more.

5 Blend Some Bubbles
With a dry Q-Tip, blend some white bubbles into the suds to soften the effect. Leave enough greys to give the bubbles depth. Accentuate the prominent bubbles with a turp brush.

6 Paint the Darks
Heavily load a small bright brush with black paint thinned to a whipped-cream consistency. Begin with the darkest areas, trying to float the black paint on top of the grey rather than stirring the grey up into the black. As the brush unloads, move to the sketchy areas, laying in strokes in the direction the fur grows. Make sure lots of grey background still shows. Scruffy puppy!

7 The Fur Pattern

Compare the fur diagram to the finished painting on page 54 and to the rough-brush photo at right. As you prepare to brush, think about how long the puppy's fur is, where it is straight or curved, and where it is dark or light. Mentally note the areas not to overwork now, as they will be extensively glowed and reworked later.

8 Rough-Brush the Fur

Gently begin to brush the ears. A light touch is essential in brushing long fur. You need little or no GEL in your bristle brush in the solid black areas. As you move into the lighter forehead and muzzle, you will need more GEL to break the paint pattern and make it blend. Clean and re-GEL your brush often in these areas.

9 Extend the Fur

Once the top of the head has been brushed, you will want to extend some wispy fur above the head. With only a few side bristles of the brush touching the canvas, lightly drag out just some tips of the head fur. Extending too much fur will re-create the crew cut, only higher, so go easy here.

You may paint in individual hairs in a few places with a tiny round brush. Now your puppy has a nice haircut but still looks like he needs a bath!

10 Glow Some Spiky Shapes
Working only one or two turped Q-Tip areas at a time, begin to re-brush and groom your puppy. Use the turped Q-Tip on its side, air-planing off the canvas to make the spiky shapes in the forehead and muzzle. Let the turp do the work! Pressure on the Q-Tip will only grind dark paint into the canvas and make it difficult to brush.

11 Re-Brush the Glowed Areas
While each glowed area still glistens with turp, brush the area in the direction the fur grows. Use a bristle brush that has been dipped in turp, blotted, and then moistened in GEL. You want just enough turp in the brush to create grey streaks and fur marks, yet not make a mush. Avoid areas you wish to remain bright white.

Repeat this glow and re-brush process as many times as needed. Long-haired pups take lots of grooming on canvas, too! When the fur is almost perfect, add a few individual hairs with a turp brush for accent.

Painting the Toy Duck

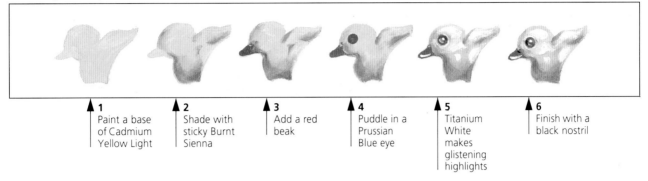

1 Paint a base of Cadmium Yellow Light

2 Shade with sticky Burnt Sienna

3 Add a red beak

4 Puddle in a Prussian Blue eye

5 Titanium White makes glistening highlights

6 Finish with a black nostril

Painting the Pup's Eye and Nose

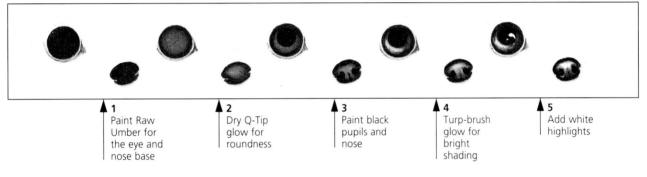

1 Paint Raw Umber for the eye and nose base

2 Dry Q-Tip glow for roundness

3 Paint black pupils and nose

4 Turp-brush glow for bright shading

5 Add white highlights

12 Final Touches
Paint and glow your pup's pink tongue, adding a few turp-brush hairs over it to set it into the muzzle.

You may choose to put a rubber duck in your painting for color or simply fill in the area with bubbles. There may be open places to turp-brush in a bucket rim. The most important finishing touch in this design, however, is the puppy's eyebrows.

After the eyes and nose are painted, experiment with different eyebrow hair positions using a turp brush and X-Acto knife. These hairs greatly change the expression, and you may need to lift them out and paint back over them several times before you've captured that look of bewildered innocence.

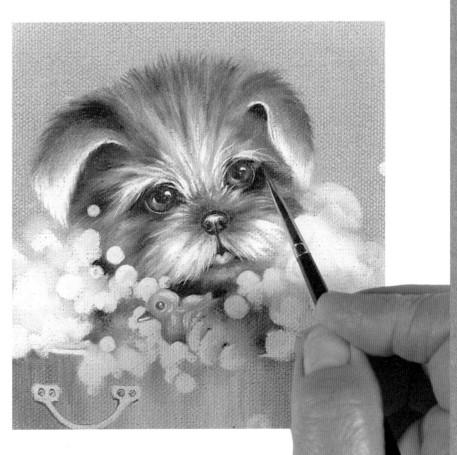

5

HOW TO PAINT
A Short-Haired Pup

"Beagle Scout"

I always say, "Put the expression on your own face when painting your animal!"
No one's looking . . . Try it! You'll be amazed how cute this pup will become as it
mirrors your expression. So, put on your big, sad eyes and pout that mouth!

What You'll Need
- Oil paints—*GEL, Titanium White, Ivory Black, Raw Umber, Cadmium Yellow Light, Sap Green, Red, Burnt Sienna*
- Mix these colors—*Background grey, deep fawn, grass green*
- Canvas—*with prepared background*
- Brushes—*small bristle round, tiny sable round, small sable bright, medium sable bright*
- X-Acto knife
- Q-Tips, cotton balls, soft paper towels
- Odorless thinner

Before You Begin
1. Using the stencil drawing on the previous page, cut a stencil or trace a line drawing of the image.
2. Transfer the image to your prepared wet background.

NOTE: *Grass may be graphite-transferred after the painting is dry.*

1 Lift out Whites
Lift out the wet grey paint from the kerchief, tail tip, feet and legs, eyes, eyebrows, muzzle and forehead, neck and chin, and fire flame. You may use a stencil and turped paper towel, a turped Q-Tip, or a turp brush. If you use a stencil, notice the areas you will still need to clear by hand.

If you use a line drawing transfer, be sure to remove all grey from the kerchief so it will not contaminate and dull the bright red paint you'll be using there later. Be prepared!

2 Paint the Darks

Using Raw Umber thinned to the consistency of whipped cream and a small bright brush, paint the shadows and dark brown fur areas. It is always helpful to compare the darks in the paint pattern to the darks in the finished painting (see page 62). Use heavier paint where the color remains darkest in the finished painting.

3 Scrumble in Color

Mix a deep fawn color by adding more Raw Umber and Burnt Sienna to our basic fawn color, or by using less yellow.

With loose, squiggly strokes, scrumble in the deep fawn paint. Remember that large S shapes with lots of grey background still showing work best. In places where you want the beagle to have even redder color, scrumble in Burnt Sienna, floating it on top of the other colors.

To paint the black saddle, heavily load a medium-sized bright brush with whipped-cream paint. The paint should fall off the brush easily. Use a very light touch to prevent stirring up grey background paint into your black.

4 The Fur Pattern

Compare this fur diagram to the finished painting on page 62 and to the rough brush in the photo below. Take note of how the fur grows out and over the face, down the ears and back, and out to the paws and tail.

Keep in mind that beagles have very short, sleek fur so you will want a shallow angle of the hairs as they pop off the edges of the image. Notice that only the tips of the hairs show on the rounded hip, because you are looking straight down the hair shafts.

5 Rough-Brush the Fur

After moistening your bristle brush in GEL, begin to brush the beagle's head. Start layering at the top of the head and work down toward the muzzle. Next, carefully brush the ear edges. Begin layering the ear fur at the bottom, working upward and finally blending it into the top of the head. Keep the head and ear fur very short. Don't over-work areas that will be destroyed later by glowing and re-brushing.

Being sure you clean and re-GEL your brush frequently, begin to layer the fur around your beagle's body. Brush the black saddle last, using almost no pressure and very little GEL. Vigorous brushing here will stir up grey paint and change your puppy into an old dog!

6 Glow Some Areas

With a turped Q-Tip or a turp brush, begin to glow and re-brush one or two areas of your beagle at a time. Keep in mind that you should remove a larger area than the finished highlight. Begin with the large, easy glow areas like the hip or ear. This will make you feel as though you are really making progress and prepare you for the more difficult facial highlights.

7 Re-Brush and Groom

Starting at the outer rim of each glowed area, carefully re-brush toward the center. Keep the bristle brush clean and GEL'ed as needed. Remember that the GEL is essential to making the fur marks, as it keeps the paint from floating shapelessly in the turpy paint ring. You may repeat this process several times until you achieve the size and brightness you desire.

Check your beagle's overall color. If necessary, add some color to the GEL in your bristle brush and directly add a bit here and there, blending as you go. You may want to enhance some facial shadows by floating deeper color on top of the fur with a small bright brush and then gently re-brushing with the bristle brush.

At this stage, anything goes! You can change and improve your puppy until it's a champion!

8 *Add Spots and Toes*

Check your beagle for any places that need cleaning up with a turp brush. Usually the facial blaze and tail can benefit from a turp-brush stroke here and there. Don't forget to clean up the kerchief edges and paint the toe marks.

NOTE: *If you'll go ahead and put in the fire's smoke now, you may let your painting dry and finish it later.*

Paint the leg, feet and face spots with fawn mixed in GEL. The GEL tranparentizes the paint and keeps the spots light. Remember that the placement of facial spots can alter your puppy's expression. You may want to change them several times.

Painting the Beagle's Eyes and Nose

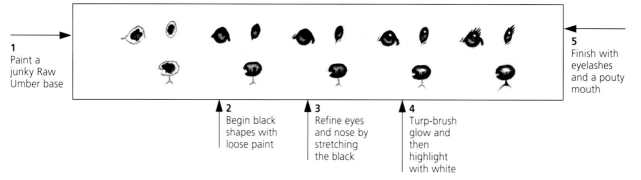

1 Paint a junky Raw Umber base

2 Begin black shapes with loose paint

3 Refine eyes and nose by stretching the black

4 Turp-brush glow and then highlight with white

5 Finish with eyelashes and a pouty mouth

Painting the Red Kerchief

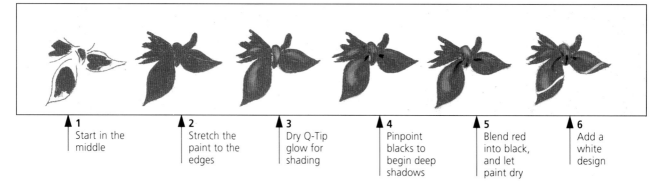

1 Start in the middle

2 Stretch the paint to the edges

3 Dry Q-Tip glow for shading

4 Pinpoint blacks to begin deep shadows

5 Blend red into black, and let paint dry

6 Add a white design

Painting the Campfire

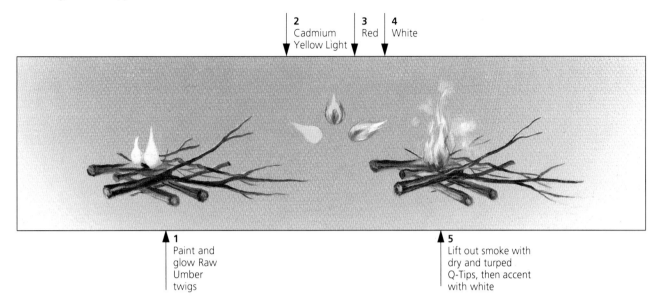

| 2 | 3 | 4 |
| Cadmium Yellow Light | Red | White |

1
Paint and glow Raw Umber twigs

5
Lift out smoke with dry and turped Q-Tips, then accent with white

9 *Final Touches*

An important part of this design is the beagle's typically woeful expression. It may take you several attempts to achieve just the right look. Don't be afraid to lift out your work and try again. Droop the eyelids, change the highlights, play with the mouth. Your turped Q-Tip and turp brush are your erasers . . . anything is possible!

When your beagle is finished, accessorize your painting with the campfire and some grass.

Making smoke with dry and turped Q-Tips is lots of fun and it's easy to create a roaring blaze before you know it. Remember, this is a baby animal, and you want to keep its world safe.

6

HOW TO PAINT
A Baby Squirrel

"Rock-a-bye Baby"

This painting really is a case of "just fiddle with it." Gorgeous, gleaming red fur will emerge from a mess—
even I am still amazed! Just keep working with it; the technique will lead the way.

What You'll Need

- Oil paints—*GEL, Titanium White, Ivory Black, Raw Umber, Cadmium Yellow Light, Burnt Sienna, Sap Green*
- Mix these colors—*background grey, fawn, grass green*
- Canvas—*with prepared background*
- Brushes—*small bristle round, tiny sable round, small sable bright, medium sable bright*
- X-Acto knife
- Q-Tips, cotton balls, soft paper towels
- Odorless thinner

Before You Begin

1. Using the stencil drawing on the previous page, cut a stencil or trace a line drawing of the image.
2. Transfer the image to your prepared wet background.

NOTE: *Pine needles are easier if painted on a dry background. You may graphite-transfer the needles then, or freehand your own.*

1 Lift out Whites

Remove the grey background from the eye, eye fur, muzzle and breast with a turped Q-Tip, turp brush, or stencil and turped paper towel. Blend the grey left under the chin into the white with a bristle brush. Brush other areas of the breast to look furry. You may have to replace some grey in the breast as you brush. With a turp brush, lift out some individual hairs on the front of the breast. Notice that these long hairs extend as far forward as the squirrel's paws.

Decide *now* how much of this image you want to work on at a time. It is easiest to finish the head and breast fur first, then the body fur, saving the branch, paws and tail for last. Paint the squirrel's eye and the pine needles when the painting is dry. This system prevents your hand from accidentally getting in wet paint and making a mess!

2 *Start With Raw Umber*

When you have decided how much of the squirrel you'll work on first, paint only that area. Proceed to brush, glow, re-brush and finish that area, then return to this step and begin the next part of your squirrel.

Start each time by painting your obvious darks and shadows with Raw Umber and a small bright brush. As the brush unloads paint, move to the sketchy, ''just for color'' strokes.

3 *Scrumble in Fawn*

Randomly scrumble in fawn over the area you are painting. Be loose, using large squiggles and leaving plenty of grey background showing through. Go easy, or by the time you're done, it won't be the wind that makes your squirrel fall from the treetop . . . it will be the weight of all that paint!

73

4 Scrumble in Burnt Sienna

Take a quick look at the rough-brush photo on page 76 (step 9). This will help orient you to where Burnt Sienna needs to be dominant. Apportion more Burnt Sienna over these areas as you paint, but scrumble it very lightly over areas you want to be less red in color.

With all this color, it's a good idea to make a shield to protect your background from accidental color smudges off your painting hand. Occasionally, some background paint will lift off when you remove the shield. Redistribute the paint by repeatedly patting it with a paper towel pad. Always wipe off the back of your shield before repositioning it.

5 Add Yellow

It is essential to thin your yellow paint to soupy, but not runny, consistency. Heavily load a medium bright brush with this yellow. Letting the paint fall off the brush, float yellow over the other colors. The yellow is responsible for the vibrant highlights of the squirrel's fur. Be sure to place yellow on all areas that will be glowed, trying not to stir up underlying paint.

6 ***Paint the Branch***
Paint the branch with a bright brush. Hold the brush at right angles to the branch, painting streaks of Raw Umber and fawn that have been diluted with varying amounts of GEL as you go. The GEL, combined with a slight wavy motion of the brush, produces a simple bark effect easily. A continuous long stroke along the branch with a bristle brush adds even more detail. Make sure the bark lines follow through correctly behind the squirrel's feet.

7 ***Add the Squirrel's Paws***
Add some GEL to a small amount of Raw Umber to paint the paws. This not only lightens the color, it makes it easy to glow individual knuckles later. Use a small bright brush on its back corner. Where there is a knuckle, or at the ends of the toes, simply pause and press the brush slightly. This will automatically create the bony look you want.

8 *The Fur Pattern*

As you compare this fur diagram to the finished painting on page 70 and to the rough-brush photo below, take particular note of how the fur sweeps back across the cheek and nut pouch. Fur on squirrels is short on the face, longer on the body, and very long on the tail. Since this is a baby, its fur is thinner and wispier than an adult's. To make the tail fluffy, the fur must pop almost straight out, leaving only the tips of the hair visible in some places.

9 *Rough-Brush the Fur*

Moisten your bristle brush sparingly with GEL. This design may require less GEL in the rough brush than usual. After brushing the major edges of the area you're working on, begin to layer the fur around your squirrel. When you brush the tail, make many fur layers to keep it bushy. Also, keep it small and thick for now.

To hold correct color levels in the fur, brush from the Burnt Sienna/yellow areas *into* the Raw Umber areas. This ensures a reddish squirrel rather than a dark brown squirrel. Always clean and re-GEL your brush after brushing Raw Umber so as not to "travel" the darks. The object is to blend but not destroy the hundreds of different shades and values you create as you brush.

10 *Glow Some Areas*
Glow small areas in the ear and paws with a turp brush. In other areas, a dry Q-Tip will gently shade and blend or remove excess paint. Try a dry Q-Tip on the nose and muzzle, gently rubbing until they look soft. Perhaps you'll need to lighten the rib-cage fur.

When glowing with a turped Q-Tip, lift and re-brush only one highlight at a time. For best results, you'll need to re-brush the glowed area before the turp evaporates.

11 *Re-Brush the Glowed Areas*
Re-brushing reddish animals is a bit tricky. You may have miscalculated the color load or overbrushed a highlight and have to paint, rough-brush, glow or re-brush a highlight several times. For a really vibrant highlight, remember to use enough yellow. Adequate turp in the Q-Tip, and GEL in the brush, also play a vital part. You should have enough turp for the highlight to glisten and enough GEL to keep the brush marks from mushing. It doesn't matter what you did, or how many times you did it over. In this method, nobody will know you weren't perfect the first time!

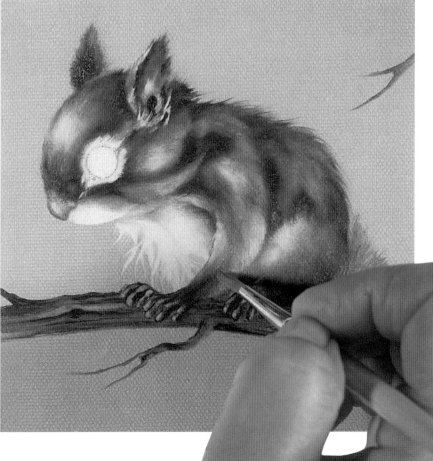

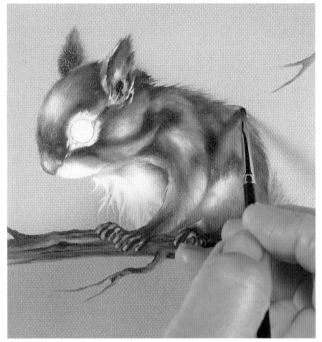

12 *Stretch out Some Back Hairs*
With a small bright brush and no paint, pull a few wispy hairs off the back to look like the wind is blowing the fur.

13 *Extend Some Tail Fur*
With more GEL than usual in the bristle brush, stretch the tail fur. To prevent "snowplowing," grab color from only the tips of the tail fur.

14 *Add Ear Highlights*
Add more highlights to the ear with a small turp brush. Turp-brush a few hairs at the base.

15 *Clean the Eye Fur*
Make sure the fur around the eye is white and the shape of the eye space is round.

16 *Glow the Paws*
Check the paws one final time, making any adjustments, and glow them. Go easy on the claws—this is a baby!

17 *Add More Tail Glow*
Make glistening tail hairs with a small bright turp brush. Airplane off smoothly for fine tips.

Painting the Eye

When your painting is dry, you can finish it without fear of mistakes. Since a light touch with a turped Q-Tip or a turp brush "erases" almost any problem, this is the time to go for perfection. The dry surface also enables you to get crisp, sharp edges.

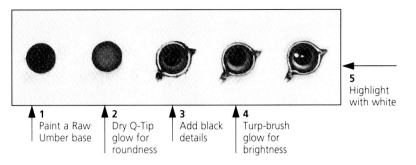

1 Paint a Raw Umber base
2 Dry Q-Tip glow for roundness
3 Add black details
4 Turp-brush glow for brightness
5 Highlight with white

Painting the Pine Needles

Pine needles are also best painted after the painting is dry. For really springy needles, try painting with your arm, not your fingers. Keep a stiff wrist, guiding the brushstroke from your shoulder. Starting at the base of the needles, pause . . . look where you're going (not where you've been) . . . and begin the stroke with steadily decreasing pressure. As you airplane off the canvas, a beautiful, tapered needle will be left behind.

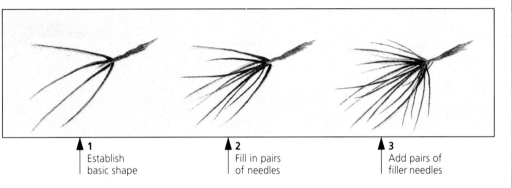

1 Establish basic shape
2 Fill in pairs of needles
3 Add pairs of filler needles

18 **Final Touches**
Paint some whisker dots on your baby squirrel and scratch out the whiskers with an X-Acto knife. Now his twitchy little nose can smell all the pine needles as he gently rocks high in his tree.

A baby fox or an Irish Setter pup would be a fun project using the techniques you've learned in this project. Red fur is always a challenge, but well worth the effort each time you capture these beautiful creatures on canvas.

7

HOW TO PAINT
A Downy Duckling

"The Promise"

I was elated the day I discovered how to make yellow fluff. For me,
this never-ending quest for new solutions is the real joy of being an artist. Every day there's something
I'm still improving—something yet to learn. Best of all . . . the journey never ends.

What You'll Need

- Oil paints—*GEL, Titanium White, Ivory Black, Raw Umber, Cadmium Yellow Light, Burnt Sienna, Red, Sap Green*
- Mix these colors—*background grey, GEL'ed yellow, deep yellow, fawn, pink*
- Canvas—*with prepared background*
- Brushes—*small bristle round, tiny sable round, small sable bright, medium sable bright*
- Special—*heavy coated paper for an egg stencil*
- X-Acto knife
- Q-Tips (more of them than usual), cotton balls, soft paper towels
- Odorless thinner

Before You Begin

1. Using the stencil drawing on the previous page, cut a stencil or trace a line drawing of the image.
2. Read Step 1, "Lift out Whites," before transferring the image to your prepared wet background. This design is especially suited to using the stencil because of the extensive lift-out of grey required. Whether using a line drawing transfer or stencil, you will need a separate stencil of just the egg.

NOTE: *Either graphite-transfer or freehand the grass after the painting is dry.*

1 Lift out Whites

Lift out the background grey from the butterfly, eye, eye feathers, feather by the egg, and major light areas of the duckling. Use a turped Q-Tip, a turp brush, or a stencil with a turped paper towel.

With a dry cotton ball, remove as little grey as possible from the egg while still being able to see its shape. Make sure the beak has been turped out so it rests on the egg.

Remove most of the remaining grey in the duck with a dry Q-Tip. This is necessary to prevent the duckling from turning green when yellow is painted on it. Lift out some soft swells in the ground using a dry cotton ball.

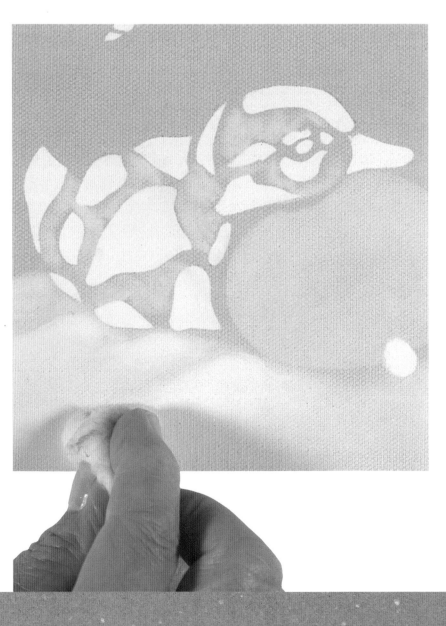

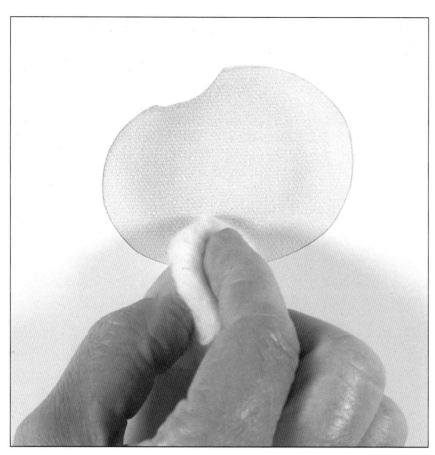

2 Lift out and Shape the Egg

Using a stencil to aid in the egg lift-outs is well worth the time spent cutting it. Be as accurate as possible so that your egg will have crisp edges when finished. With a dry cotton ball, lift out areas you want whiter. As with all spherical shapes, the darkest areas will be somewhat toward the middle of the shape, *not* on the extreme edges. This is due to the light's flowing around the curved surface. Using a light touch and a continuously clean side of the cotton ball is a must.

3 Highlight the Egg

For a bright highlight on your egg, lift out an area larger than the finished highlight with a turped Q-Tip. Carefully blend this area by placing a dry cotton ball in the center of the turped shape and gently moving the cotton ball in small concentric circles. Keep pressure on the center of the cotton ball only. This will prevent a hard edge from forming around your highlighted area.

NOTE: *You may stop at this stage and continue working tomorrow, or hold your painting wrapped in plastic in your freezer for up to two weeks before proceeding.*

4 ***Start With Yellow***
Heavily load a medium bright brush with the GEL'ed yellow. Being careful of the image's outline, paint the thick mixture over the duckling, avoiding shadow areas behind the head, on the neck and under the wing. You will be able to see paint ridges left by the brush, but don't make it too gloppy.

NOTE: *At this point your painting will hold overnight at room temperature and still be workable the next day.*

5 ***Add Darks and Shadows***
Paint the darks and shadows with a small bright brush. Compare the paint pattern to the finished painting on page 80 and to the rough-brush photo on page 86. As you do this, notice how much of the "yellow" duckling is really other colors. Since lights do not look light without darks, contrast is essential. The next few steps will be a test of faith. Your duckling will look yellow again—just not for now!

6 Scrumble in Fawn

Scrumble fawn into areas you wish to result in midtone shadows. Although the fawn paint doesn't cover large areas, it is relatively heavy paint where it is used. Next, randomly unload the brush in a few other places. This will result in some incidental tones to give the duckling's down more depth.

Sufficient fawn color is important because it keeps the Burnt Sienna subtle and prevents your Easter duckling from looking like a Halloween pumpkin!

7 Add Burnt Sienna

Compare the rough-brush photo on page 86 to the paint pattern in places you will be painting Burnt Sienna. When you rough-brush your duckling, the Burnt Sienna will blend with the yellow and fawn and create a variety of shades automatically. When the duckling is glowed, even more shades will appear. The deep color of the rough-brushed duckling indicates you should be laying down good, strong color at this stage.

8 The Feather Pattern

Although the down of a duckling is basically just fuzz, it will help retain some semblance of reality if you approximate the direction of the feathers when they grow in. Relate this diagram to the finished painting on page 80, paying special attention to the extra-fluffy areas. Observe that a duckling head is not round like a baby chick's. Imagine touching the baby-soft down.

9 Rough-Brush the Down

GEL will not be necessary in your bristle brush at this time because it's already mixed in the yellow. Carefully brush the edges of the duckling, keeping the feathers short for now. You will extend some edges later.

Rapidly layer feathers, wiping your bristle brush frequently and using almost no pressure on the brush. Be especially careful not to travel too much Raw Umber into other areas. Neatness is not a priority here, since turp-glowing and re-brushing will alter much of this rough-brushing.

10 *Glow Some Areas*

Working the large major highlights first, remove several glow areas at a time with turped Q-Tips. Re-brush each highlight before the turp you deposited evaporates. Work as cleanly as possible. Yellow has a nasty habit of enveloping the canvas, you, and the studio. You will be glowing each highlighted area more than once, so have lots of Q-Tips and a big wastebasket ready!

11 *Re-Brush*

GEL is particularly essential in this design to achieve the soft look of the duckling down. Clean and re-moisten your bristle brush with GEL often. Due to the heavy paint, you will have to glow and re-brush each highlight several times. Glow and re-brush the entire duckling once before beginning to re-work any areas. Gradually, the color of the entire duckling will appear to lighten as you remove areas and re-blend them. Leave very bright white centers in the final glowed areas.

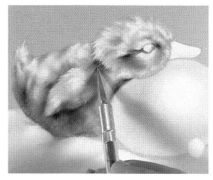

12 *Add Color*
Some areas may require added color for richness. Apply deep yellow directly with the bristle brush, blending as you go.

13 *Accent Feathers*
With a small turp brush and/or X-Acto knife, accentuate some feathers on the back of the head, wing and tail.

14 *Puddle in the Eye*
Puddle in a black, beady eye, shade the surrounding feathers, and add a droplet of white for the eye highlights.

Painting the Feather
Once the feather is done, allow your painting to dry before finishing it.

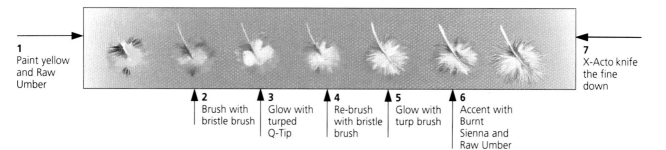

1
Paint yellow and Raw Umber

2
Brush with bristle brush

3
Glow with turped Q-Tip

4
Re-brush with bristle brush

5
Glow with turp brush

6
Accent with Burnt Sienna and Raw Umber

7
X-Acto knife the fine down

15 *Add Color to·the Egg*
Dip a dry cotton ball in a bit of fawn. Smudge the paint over the cotton ball by rubbing it on a paper towel. With just a "stain" of paint left on the cotton ball, lightly rub areas of the egg to be shaded. Use your egg stencil to protect the rest of the painting. Repeat, using a touch of Burnt Sienna.

16 *Add Spots to the Egg*
With small brushes, add some spots to the egg. Adding GEL to fawn or Raw Umber makes the spots appear translucent. Vary the size and proximity of the spots to each other for a more realistic effect.

Painting the Duckling's Beak

Both the beak and the butterfly should be painted with a sheer base of paint thinned only enough to allow it to spread evenly. Burnt Sienna is best applied very sticky and then blended with a thoroughly wiped-out brush. Do not dip it in turp—just wipe it out. Whipped-cream-consistency white will float over this base easily. Use a heavily loaded brush and no pressure as you stroke.

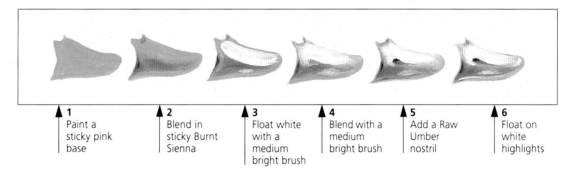

1 Paint a sticky pink base

2 Blend in sticky Burnt Sienna

3 Float white with a medium bright brush

4 Blend with a medium bright brush

5 Add a Raw Umber nostril

6 Float on white highlights

Painting the Butterfly

1 Paint a sticky Cadmium Yellow Light base

2 Blend in Burnt Sienna

3 Float on white accents

4 Add pink spots

5 Use soupy fawn for body and spots

6 Float a white eye and spots

17 Final Touches

Anchor your duckling and egg with a few blades of grass. Remember to heavily load your brush with loose paint and use airplane strokes for the prettiest tips. Pulling blades up through the downy feather is fun. Imagine the blades underneath the feather before you pull them through and it will almost seem as if you're watching them grow. Spring has sprung!

8

HOW TO PAINT
A Tabby Kitten

"Purrmanent Press!"

Sometimes a really cute title comes to me and I just have to paint it. Other times,
I'll see something cute happen, like my cat's fascination with a belligerent toad.
Of course, all of nature isn't cute, but for those of us who love
and paint baby animals, it's a big part of it.

What You'll Need

- Oil paints—*GEL, Titanium White, Ivory Black, Raw Umber, Burnt Sienna, Cadmium Yellow Light, Red*
- Mix these colors—*Background grey, light Burnt Sienna, dark pink, fawn*
- Special—*a small fan brush (optional)*
- Canvas—*with prepared background*
- Brushes—*small bristle round, tiny sable round, small sable bright, medium sable bright*
- X-Acto knife
- Q-Tips, cotton balls, soft paper towels
- Odorless thinner

Before You Begin

1. Using the stencil drawing on the previous page, cut a stencil or trace a line drawing of the image.
2. Transfer the image to your prepared wet background.

NOTE: *A stencil is very helpful in this design for quick removal of grey in the large white areas of the laundry.*

1 Lift out Whites

Using a stencil and turped paper towel, a turped Q-Tip or a turp brush, lift out the grey background from the muzzle, eyes, eye fur, forehead stripes, paws, and major areas of the laundry. Remember that a turped towel, Q-Tip, or brush will put lifted paint (or "dirt") back on the canvas as fast as it lifted it out. Change or clean tools often for a sparkling white laundry!

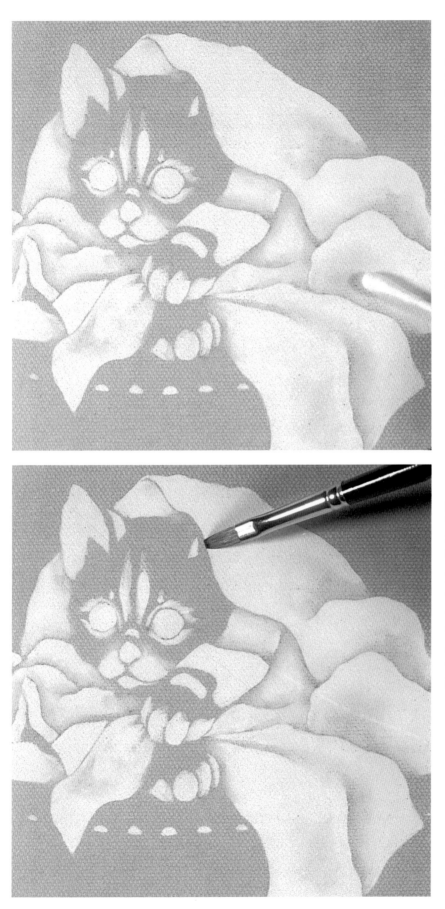

2 Blend the Shadows

To begin blending the shadow areas of the laundry, use a clean turped Q-Tip that you have thoroughly blotted out on a paper towel. With no pressure, stroke the line where the grey shadow area meets the white laundry. The small amount of turp you've deposited on this line will help you blend the grey shadow smoothly into the white with a dry Q-Tip. For best effects, use the dry Q-Tip on its side with gradual, even pressure. In some areas, you may have to paint in some grey and then blend with a dry Q-Tip.

3 Clean up Edges

For crisp edges of the laundry shapes, run a turp brush along all the edges, holding the brush at right angles to the line you are cleaning up.

NOTE: *At this point, your painting will hold overnight and still be workable tomorrow. Or, carefully wrap your painting in plastic and hold it in your freezer for up to two weeks, because you probably have real laundry to do!*

4 *Start With Burnt Sienna*

After you have added pink to the ears and softened them with a dry Q-Tip, begin painting the Burnt Sienna pattern with your small bright brush. Go easy, because there's a lot of painting left to do!

Either paint in the stitching, button, and buttonhole details of the laundry now, or wait until the painting is dry. Dry is easier, since you can turp out any mistakes.

5 *Scrumble Light Burnt Sienna and Fawn*

With whipped-cream-consistency light Burnt Sienna and fawn, scrumble strokes more or less going in the direction the fur grows. Keep the paint sketchy and leave lots of grey background showing. You can always add more color later if you need to. Avoid using Burnt Sienna paint in the fur disappearing under the laundry. Carefully tapping in a little fawn along these lines is safer.

6 *Add Yellow*

Thin your yellow to soupy but not runny consistency. Heavily load a medium bright brush and, letting the paint fall off the brush, float yellow throughout the kitty. Try not to let any yellow or sienna get on your laundry, since even bleach won't get the stains out!

7 **The Fur Pattern**
Study this fur diagram and compare it to the finished painting on page 90 and to the rough-brush photo below. Notice the fur is brushed upward on the paws to make them look fluffier. Fur growing inside the ear not only grows from the head upward, but also from the side of the ear. Go look at a real kitty and study its ear fur.

8 **Rough-Brush the Fur**
Always staying well away from your laundry, begin to brush the kitty's fur with your bristle brush. Think about the length of the fur and stroke in the direction the fur grows . . . but don't overwork at this stage. Once the fur is roughly brushed, cautiously sneak the bristle brush to within a few hairlines of the laundry laying over the kitty. Any further brushing here is best done with a small bright brush.

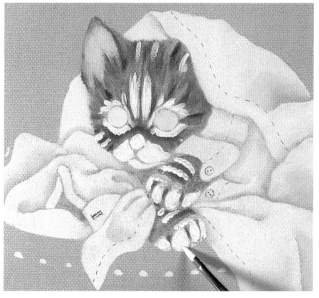

9 **Paint the White Areas**
With a turped Q-Tip or turp brush, remove any excess paint from areas of the kitty that should be white when finished. Using whipped-cream-consistency white, and letting the paint fall off the heavily loaded bright brush, put paint on the white areas. Try not to let the brush hairs touch the canvas or stir up any other color.

10 Brush the White Areas

Brush the white paint areas with a bristle brush and a very light touch. Avoid the bright white centers as much as possible. If the entire area becomes dingy, you can always lift it out with a turped Q-Tip and begin again. To ''frost'' the rest of the fur, directly add some white with the bristle brush as you re-brush and groom your kitty.

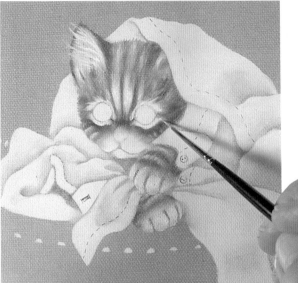

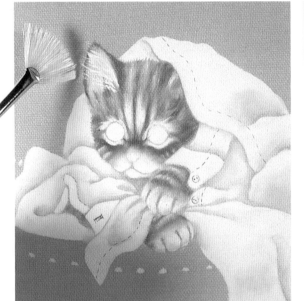

11 Add Fur to the Ears

A small fan brush is a good way to add silky, long fur in the ears. Add just a few stray hairs with a tiny round brush.

12 Clean Up

Search for places to improve your kitty. Perhaps it needs more dark around the eyes. To adjust overly red areas, brush in a bit of fawn.

Painting the Eye

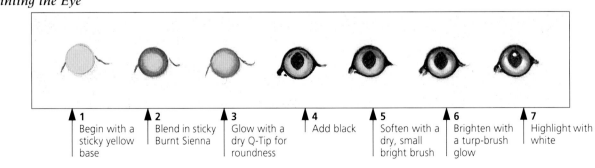

1 Begin with a sticky yellow base

2 Blend in sticky Burnt Sienna

3 Glow with a dry Q-Tip for roundness

4 Add black

5 Soften with a dry, small bright brush

6 Brighten with a turp-brush glow

7 Highlight with white

Painting the Pink Nose

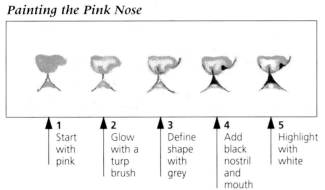

1 Start with pink **2** Glow with a turp brush **3** Define shape with grey **4** Add black nostril and mouth **5** Highlight with white

13 *Scratch out Some Whiskers*
Finish bringing your kitty to life with some long, graceful whiskers. An X-Acto knife is perfect for this.

Painting the Basket

Begin the basket with a medium shade (fawn mixed with white). Establish the wicker ribs and rim. Next, shade in Raw Umber shadows, followed by white highlights. Continue to dab in colors until the basket has a "wickery" texture.

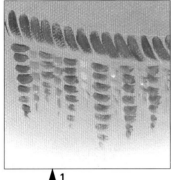

1 Begin with fawn mixed with white   **2** Accent with Raw Umber   **3** Continue to weave basket with paint

14 *Final Touches*
To give yourself lots of time in this design, you may want to paint the basket, nose and eyes when your painting is dry. This will also allow you to "erase" mistakes easily with a Q-Tip or turp brush. Part of the fun of this entire technique is that you don't always have to be right the first time!

Kitty eyes are among the most difficult of all eyes to paint well. They require a steady hand and lots of patience. Matching the diamond-shaped pupils can be particularly frustrating. Perhaps you'll want to rehearse a few times on scrap canvas. It's true: Practice makes purrfect!

9

HOW TO PAINT
A Long-Haired Kitten

"Ribbon 'n Blues"

White Persian cats have incredible fur. Depicting its exquisite feathery feel is
always a challenge. Combining that with luminous eyes and shining ribbons will really
test your skills. I had a patient model—"Co Co"—a creature of unbelievable beauty.

What You'll Need

- Oil paints—*GEL, Titanium White, Ivory Black, Prussian Blue, Red, Sap Green*
- Mix these colors—*background grey, dark grey, dark blue, medium blue, blue-green, pink, oiled white (white thinned with linseed oil until soupy but not runny)*
- Special—*linseed oil, fan brush*
- Optional—*Cobalt drier*
- Canvas—*with prepared background*
- Brushes—*small bristle round, tiny sable round, small sable bright, medium sable bright*
- X-Acto knife
- Q-Tips, cotton balls, soft paper towels
- Odorless thinner

Before You Begin

1. Using the stencil drawing on the previous page, cut a stencil or trace a line drawing of the image.
2. Transfer the image to your prepared wet background.

NOTE: *In the line drawing and stencil, the fur is not extended beyond the head as far as it will be in the finished painting. This avoids harsh marks in the finished fur tips.*

1 Lift out Whites

Lift out the grey background from the outer ears, forehead, eyes, eye fur, nose, muzzle and ribbon. Use a turped Q-Tip, a turp brush, or a stencil and turped paper towel. Very careful lifting-out of the eye shapes and surrounding fur will be helpful later.

Add pink to the inner ear with a dry Q-Tip. Gently smudge the pink over the grey, leaving some grey in the base of the ear and around the rim of the ear. With a clean Q-Tip, lighten the tip of the inner ear slightly, leaving enough color to contrast with the white fur you'll be adding later.

2 *The Fur Pattern*

Take a long time comparing this fur diagram to the finished painting on page 98. Long-haired kitties have very short outer ear and facial fur. Be aware of how wispy the tips of the longer fur look as they extend beyond the undercoat. Notice that even where fur is very long, it is still composed of many, many layers. In some places only the tips are visible, as the fur stands straight out toward you.

3 *Start Shaping the Fur*

Using a turped Q-Tip on its side, lay in shapes that approximate the shape and direction of clumps of fur. Make teardrop shapes by slightly jiggling the Q-Tip in place and then airplaning off the canvas. Your kitty now resembles a jigsaw puzzle with a few pieces missing.

4 *Rough-Brush the Fur*

Dip your bristle brush in turp and lightly blot it on a paper towel. It should retain just enough turp to produce "hair" streaks as you brush your kitty with a back-and-forth scrubbing stroke. This step produces a good base for your painting. It also lets you begin to establish areas of light and shadow out of the maze of white shapes.

NOTE: *At this stage, you may hold your painting overnight and continue tomorrow, or hold it wrapped in plastic in the freezer for up to two weeks.*

5 Brush in White Paint

With unthinned, stiff white paint, tap white on the short fur areas of the kitty with a bristle brush. It should look stippled and furry. With oiled paint and a fan brush, fill in the long hair in the correct directions. For now, keep your layers of fur shorter than the finished fur will be.

NOTE: *You may wish to add just a few tiny drops of cobalt drier to the white and the oiled white paint. Otherwise, this painting takes several weeks to dry.*

6 Blend the Fur

Using dry cotton balls, softly blend and then slightly extend the long fur. Very gently, pat and rub the facial fur so it is lightly blended. Ignore the eyes and nose . . . they'll still show through the sheer coating of white.

7 Re-Brush With White Paint

Reapply stiff white paint to the short fur areas with your bristle brush. Study the fur diagram and finished painting once more to check your fur's direction, length and angles. The whole process may seem futile as you destroy and replace layers of paint, but you are gradually building more realistic-looking fur than a single application can achieve.

8 Add Grey Shadows

To make your whites look highlighted, you'll need to "reverse-glow" the kitty by adding dark grey shadow areas with the bristle brush. Remember: You achieve the illusion of form in light animals by using more darks than you might think possible!

9 Blend the Greys

As you blend the dark greys with the bristle brush, you will automatically create an entire range of grey values. Don't be afraid to leave the deepest shadow areas very dark. At this point, your kitty should look like it's been playing underneath the car!

10 Brush out the Longest Hairs

With a feather-light touch, begin to add the final longest hairs with a small fan brush and oiled white paint. Pay careful attention to the direction and curve of these long hairs. Keep the fur a bit short at first. Gradually extend the length of each layer of fur with successive applications of paint. Some places will groom best with a clean fan brush and no paint. Always airplane off the canvas to make delicate fur tips.

11 Enhance the Details

Accent your kitty's fur with a few individual hairs painted with a tiny round brush. Paint a few individual hairs in the ears for a slightly tangled effect. Perfect the fur around the eyes and muzzle. Thoroughly check your kitty for places you can improve. Keep fiddling until it's picture purrfect!

NOTE: *You may allow your painting to dry at this stage and finish it later.*

Painting the Eye and Nose

Begin the eyes with sheer paint so as not to have excessive buildup as you progress. Anything can be removed with turp and redone, so be particular. Shade some grey into the surrounding fur for a finished look.

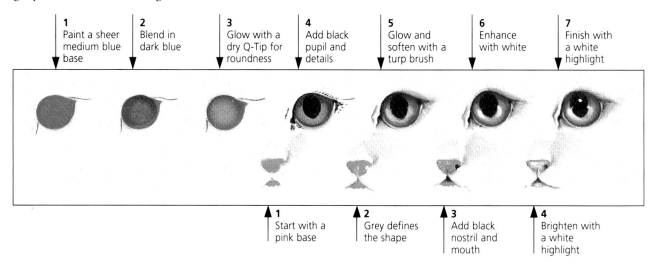

1 Paint a sheer medium blue base

2 Blend in dark blue

3 Glow with a dry Q-Tip for roundness

4 Add black pupil and details

5 Glow and soften with a turp brush

6 Enhance with white

7 Finish with a white highlight

1 Start with a pink base

2 Grey defines the shape

3 Add black nostril and mouth

4 Brighten with a white highlight

Painting the Blue Ribbon

For crisp ribbon edges, paint the middle of the shape first with a small bright brush. Dip the brush in turp, and wipe it out. Using no further paint, stretch the paint already in the shape out to the edges. This thins the paint as it approaches the edge and makes a very sharp, hard edge. Grey the blue in the neck ribbon as it approaches the chin for a shadow effect.

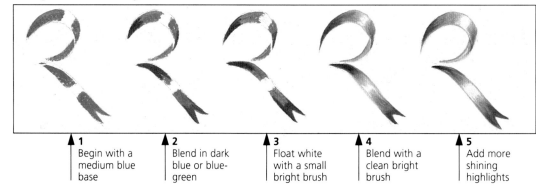

1 Begin with a medium blue base

2 Blend in dark blue or blue-green

3 Float white with a small bright brush

4 Blend with a clean bright brush

5 Add more shining highlights

12 Extend the Fur Over the Ribbon

Sink the ribbon into the fur by painting some hairs over the ribbon. Be sure to blend them into the rest of the fur.

Painting the Bell

A bell or small heart charm on the ribbon adds extra interest.

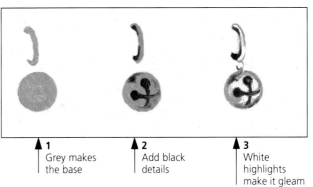

1
Grey makes the base

2
Add black details

3
White highlights make it gleam

13 Final Touches

Finish your kitty with painted whisker dots and very long, graceful whiskers scratched in with an X-Acto knife. If your painting is dry, your blade should be very sharp.

Long-haired kitties are some of the more difficult animals to paint, but they always seem worth the time and patience required. You may have to paint them many times until you feel you've really captured their incredibly soft, long, fluffy fur. Once you've mastered the fur, it's fun to paint long-haired kitties with other fur or eye colors. Try a shy grey kitty with smoky grey eyes or a calico with big orange eyes. So many possibilities . . . but one thing's for sure: Your *best* paintings are yet to come!

10

HOW TO PAINT
Baby Bunnies

"Lullabye"

Bunnies are so innocent, so vulnerable. Painting them heightens my awareness
of the fragile balance of nature and my desire to preserve and protect it. I always hope that
my depiction of one precious, fleeting moment will evoke those same feelings in others.

What You'll Need

- Oil paints—*GEL, Titanium White, Ivory Black, Raw Umber, Cadmium Yellow Light, Red, Sap Green*
- Mix these colors—*Background grey, fawn, pink, deep yellow-orange, grass green*
- Canvas—*with prepared background*
- Brushes—*small bristle round, tiny sable round, small sable bright, medium sable bright*
- X-Acto knife
- Q-Tips, cotton balls, soft paper towels
- Odorless thinner

Before You Begin

1. Using the stencil drawing on the previous page, cut a stencil or trace a line drawing of the image.
2. Transfer the image to your prepared wet background.

NOTE: *Although the clover and grass are prettier worked on a wet background, it is easier to paint when the background is dry. You may opt to do a graphite transfer of them later.*

1 Lift out Whites

Lift out the wet grey background paint from the butterflies, eyes, eye fur, foot pads, paws, tails and inner ears. Use a turped Q-Tip, a turp brush, or a stencil and turped paper towel. If you use a stencil, lift out the eye fur with a turp brush. Before you paint, put in the pink areas and soften them with a dry Q-Tip.

This is a complicated design. Take a minute now to compare your transfer to the finished painting on page 106 and to the paint pattern at right. This will ensure accuracy later.

2 **Paint the Darks**
Since this is a multi-animal design, work more precisely than usual, particularly when painting the dark areas that define shape. Painting one bunny at a time, begin with the darkest Raw Umber areas, moving to the lighter strokes as the brush unloads. Be stingy! Let the paint skip, leaving lots of grey showing.

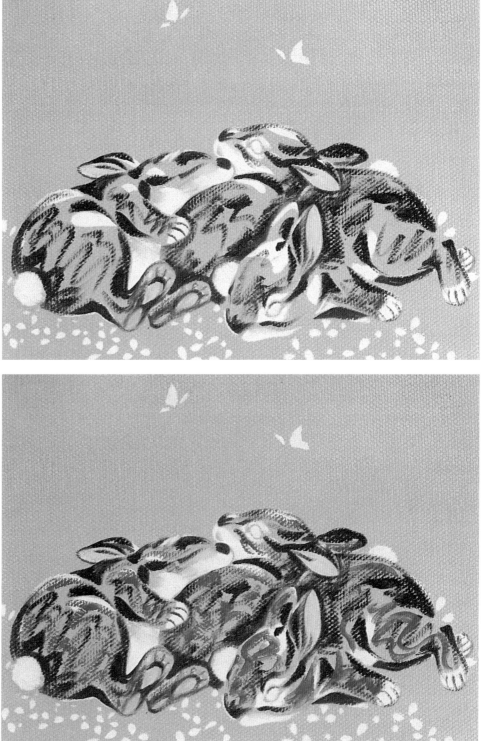

3 **Scrumble in Fawn**
Scrumble in fawn color with large squiggles, allowing the brush to fully unload before loading more paint. This results in more shades of color when the fur is brushed. There *is* a method to this madness!

4 *The Fur Pattern*

Carefully compare this fur diagram to the finished painting on page 106 and to the rough-brush photo below for fur direction guidance. It's easy to become confused with so many parts involved! Notice that the hips and bottoms are being brushed in circular patterns to make them appear very fluffy and soft.

5 *Rough-Brush the Fur*

Brush one bunny at a time, frequently wiping out your bristle brush and re-GELing it. This prevents traveling of unwanted color to other areas. As you work, imagine how soft, dense and short this fur is.

6 Glow Some Areas

With a turped Q-Tip, remove a few highlights at a time and re-brush them with a clean, GEL'ed bristle brush. As always, you may have to repeat this process several times to produce just the right shade and softness of the fur.

7 Re-Brush and Blend

To lighten fur that is too dark but doesn't require glowing, gently remove some of it with a dry Q-Tip and re-brush with GEL in your brush. Use a dry Q-Tip to soften and blend paws, muzzles and inner ears. Make sure scruffy bunnies are now groomed bunnies.

8 Glow and Soften the Feet

Clean up and glow the pads of the feet with a small turp brush, softening with a dry Q-Tip as you work.

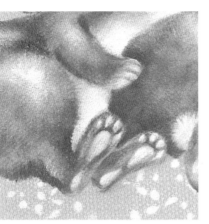

9 Brighten Some Areas

Check all other pink and white areas and perfect them as needed. Some may need a touch of white paint to brighten them.

10 Paint the Eyes and Add Some Whiskers

Puddle in the open eye and place the highlight. Take special note of the shape of the top bunny's eye. Don't forget the eyelashes and whisker dots. You may want to darken the noses and add other pinpoint dark accents to help define shapes.

Painting the Butterfly

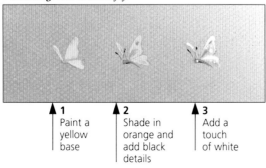

1 Paint a yellow base

2 Shade in orange and add black details

3 Add a touch of white

Painting the Clover

You may finish your painting when it is dry, although the clover leaves can be glowed better when painted on a wet background. There may be other flowers you want to nestle your bunnies in. Add your own special touches . . . make it yours!

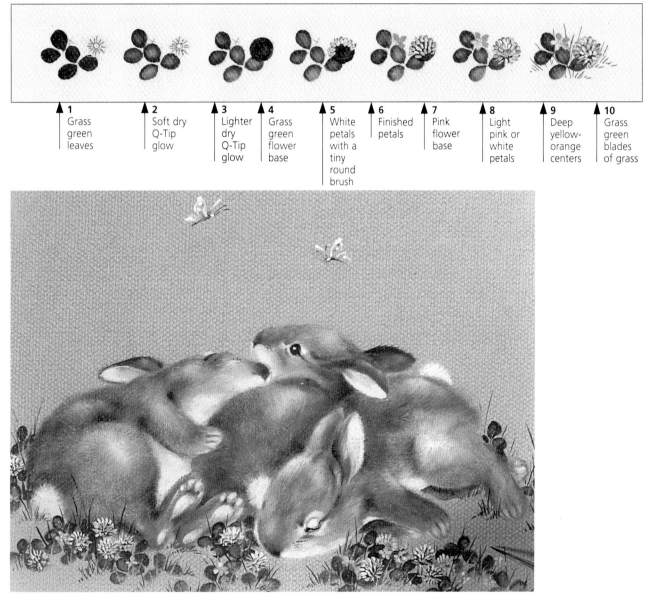

1 Grass green leaves

2 Soft dry Q-Tip glow

3 Lighter dry Q-Tip glow

4 Grass green flower base

5 White petals with a tiny round brush

6 Finished petals

7 Pink flower base

8 Light pink or white petals

9 Deep yellow-orange centers

10 Grass green blades of grass

11 *Finish*
To finish your bunnies, scratch out whiskers with an X-Acto blade and add some final, delicate blades of grass. It's always hard to resist adding "just one more." These bunnies are a lot of work, but just like children asleep at the end of the day . . . they're worth it!

harris

HOW TO PAINT
Snow Bunnies

"Peace On Earth"

Painting quiet snow scenes is as soothing as the falling snow itself. It's wonderful
to be able to create your own world every day. In the real world, though,
it's never too early to get ready for the holidays. Better start painting *now*!

What You'll Need

- Oil paints—*GEL, Titanium White, Ivory Black, Raw Umber, Burnt Sienna, Red, Sap Green*
- Mix these colors—*background grey, fawn, pink, grass green*
- Special—*An old table knife*
- Canvas—*with prepared background*
- Brushes—*small bristle round, tiny sable round, small sable bright, medium sable bright*
- X-Acto knife
- Q-Tips and cotton balls (more of them than usual), soft paper towels
- Odorless thinner

Before You Begin

1. Using the stencil drawing on the previous page, cut a stencil or trace a line drawing of the image.
2. Transfer the image to your prepared wet canvas. Keep this background as loose as possible. Excessive smoothing with the paper towel will grind in the grey paint and make it harder to lift out the snow.

NOTE: *You may wish to add some Ivory Black to the areas behind the tree and blend them in with a dry paper towel.*

1 Lift out Whites

Lift out the grey background from the insides of the ears, tail, feet, eyes, cheeks, muzzles and breast of the bunnies. Always working with a clean side of a cotton ball, begin to gently wipe out large areas of snow drifts.

As with all the lift-out tools, the cotton ball lifts paint when it is clean, and deposits lifted paint back on the canvas when it is "dirty." Pressure on the cotton ball grinds "dirt" into the canvas and makes really bright, sparkling snow impossible to achieve. Don't make another stroke without turning that cotton ball to a clean side!

2 *Brighten Some Snowdrifts*
Begin brightening selected snowdrifts by lifting out a large white area with a turped Q-Tip. The area should retain a slight glisten of turp.

3 *Blend With a Cotton Ball*
With a dry cotton ball, blend the turped area. Place the cotton ball in the middle of the turped area and gently jiggle it in small circles. Pressure on only the center of the cotton ball ensures that no hard "ring" develops. Repeat this process as needed to get bright whites.

4 *Add Some Small Drifts*
You can add small drifts with a turp brush and blend them with a dry Q-Tip. A turp brush cleans up the top edges of the drifts.

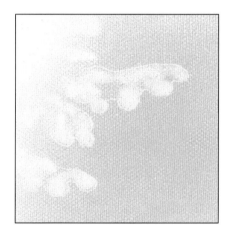

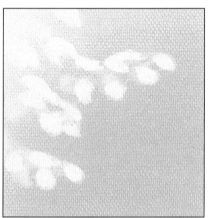

5 *Lift out Snow on the Tree*
Using a dry Q-Tip, lift out "mounds" of snow where it rests on the tree branches. Think of the form of the tree and the needles underneath the fallen snow. This will help keep your snow realistic.

6 *Highlight Some Bright Areas*
For extra-bright areas, lift out highlights with a turped Q-Tip. Gently jiggle the Q-Tip in place before enlarging a highlight area. Working over the entire tree, make fewer highlights at first than you'll want eventually. There are more shadow areas here than you may think.

7 *Blend and Soften Edges*
With a dry Q-Tip, blend some of each highlight into the surrounding snow. Connect some of the shapes for a softer, fresh-fallen snow look.

NOTE: *At this point you may stop and continue tomorrow, or hold your painting sealed in plastic in the freezer for up to two weeks.*

8 *Paint Shadows and Darks*

Paint in the ear pinks and soften them with a dry Q-Tip. Load a small bright brush with whipped-cream-consistency Raw Umber. Paint shadows and dark fur areas first. Keep careful track of when you are defining another shape with the Raw Umber. Make sure your Raw Umber strokes are leaving pretty ear and head shapes next to them. Sometimes what you're *not* painting is the place to watch. Then scrumble in some fawn for added color.

9 *The Fur Pattern*

Study this fur diagram and relate it to the rough-brush photo at the top of the facing page. Notice that the back bunny's bottom and the front bunny's hip are treated like powder puffs.

Sometimes perspective will make fur seem to grow in the wrong direction as it pops over the rounded surfaces. This is particularly true with short, fluffy fur. These bunnies are in the snow, so think about their soft, fluffed-out fur keeping them warm. Sounds weird, but it helps!

10 Rough-Brush the Fur

Brush this design with more GEL than usual moistening your bristle brush. Added GEL results in a more golden color when the animal is glowed. Brush the major edges and then layer fur around your bunnies. As these are small bunnies, work carefully. Try not to travel too much Raw Umber. Retain some grey when possible for really rich fur. The more skilled you become, the more colors you'll be able to retain in the rough-brush stage. For softly glowed areas, remove some color with dry Q-Tips and re-brush with GEL.

11 Glow Some Areas

With turped Q-Tips, glow one or two areas at a time. Jiggle the Q-Tip slightly before enlarging the turped shape. This deposits enough turp for re-brushing and also makes a more golden, vibrant highlight. Remember that the mushy turped ring of color around the bright white center is the secret to no-work, no-palette-mixing, multiple shades of color.

12 Re-Brush Fur and Refine Snow

Re-brush glowed areas with a bristle brush moistened in GEL. For the brightest highlights, clean and re-GEL the brush often. It may be difficult to maintain the bright white centers in small areas like the nose, ears and back wrinkles. This is no-fail painting, so just remove and re-brush the highlight again . . . and again, if needed.

Refine the snow around the bunnies with a turp brush. Cover any stains with a dab of white paint, blending it into the bare canvas with a dry Q-Tip.

Now . . . are your bunnies groomed and your snow sparkling?

13 Add Eyes and Whiskers

Puddle in an eye on the top bunny, stirring and stretching the puddle until it's the correct size and shape. Add a small turp glow, some eyelashes, and a white highlight.

Check for any white fur that may need cleaning with a small turp brush. Shade in and finish the sleeping bunny's eye and toes. You may want to add some darker grey beneath the bunny for contrast. Add whisker dots and scratch out the whiskers with an X-Acto knife.

Either now or when your painting is dry, check for places that would benefit from a touch of darker color. Try a few well-placed pinpoint blacks in deep shadow areas.

NOTE: *You may let your painting dry now and finish it later.*

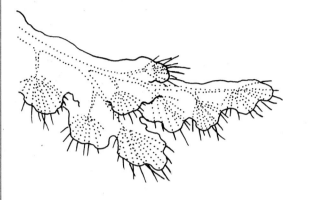

14 *Pine Needle Diagram*
Study this diagram to better understand how the needles will be peeking out from under the snow. This will prevent small green "pocket combs" from being stuck on the bottom of snow mounds.

15 *Paint the Pine Needles*
Paint needles under some of the snow mounds, always thinking of the angle of the needle as it pops from the hidden branch and out through the snow.

16 *Flick on Snowflakes*
Make snowflakes by thinning your white paint to soupy, but not runny, consistency. Be sure to get out all the lumps. Load your bristle brush with paint and unload it slightly on a table knife. Practice flicking the bristles of the brush on the edge of the knife to create spatters of snowflakes. Once you've discovered the right combination of "flick" and paint to create the size and number of flakes you want, begin making snow on the painting.

Be cautious . . . you don't want your bunnies to get lost in a blizzard!

OOOPS! NOW WHAT?

We'll fix it—that's what! Here are some very common problems, what caused them and how to correct them. This really is no-fail painting!

PROBLEMS	SOLUTIONS

TRANSFERRING

Turp bleeds You used too much turp or pressure on the paper towel in lifting out a stencil (it's as if you squeezed out a sponge).

Blot the excess turp with a paper towel pad. Smudge the background back in with your finger and smooth it with a paper towel. Reapply the stencil if you lose your image.

LIFTING OUT WHITES

Highlight won't blend There was not enough turp in the Q-Tip lift-out, or the turp evaporated. Perhaps you put too much pressure on the cotton ball while blending and absorbed the turp before the blending was complete.

Repeat the process. You've got lots of chances to make it perfect!

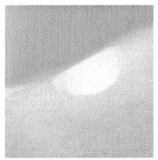

Blotchy blending You applied uneven pressure on the Q-Tip.

Don't just concentrate on the technique . . . watch what you're creating as you work. Gradually and evenly decrease or increase pressure on the Q-Tip from light to dark. Break the hard line between grey and white with a small amount of turp before blending with a dry Q-Tip.

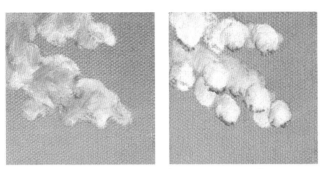

Lighten your pressure, and change Q-Tips much more often. This will absorb the dirt, rather than deposit it.

"Dirty," or ringed, Q-Tip lift-outs Using a dirty Q-Tip and too much pressure transformed your Q-Tip into a dirty sponge.

Snowplowed grey ring Not airplaning strokes with a bristle or turp brush caused the turpy paint to accumulate in front of the brush.

Erase the ring by airplaning back into the white with a bristle brush. Clean your brush after each stroke.

PAINTING FUR

Partially remove the paint with a dry Q-Tip (in the painting or brushing stage). Re-brush with GEL and you're back on track!

Animal is too dark The brushstrokes in this animal were too wide, the paint was too deep, or the paint was too sticky. (A "heavy hand" on the brush will create a very dark animal when the fur is brushed.)

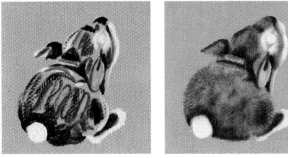

No need to be so timid. It won't bite! Re-paint and re-brush, or directly add color (mixed with GEL) with a bristle brush. This is an easy fix!

Animal is too light Brushstrokes were too thin and the paint was not deep enough. Skimpy use of paint or paint that was too turpy has made your animal look washed out.

UNRECOGNIZABLE ANIMALS

Careless painting of dark shadows (neck wrinkles), too much paint (width of strokes and depth of paint all over), hairlining outside the lines (nose and foot), and bad negative shapes (inside ear) are all evident here.

First, lift out excess paint and re-brush with GEL. Clean up the ear and whites with a turp brush. Re-brush the edge fur with drag-in strokes (clean your brush after each stroke). Practice this stage before glowing, and be more deliberate next time. You were just a little over-eager.

Careless brushing of a careless paint job magnifies the problem. Common mistakes seen here are: too much GEL, fur brushed out too long (all over), wrong fur directions (face), bad rotation of fur (hip), uneven brushing of edge fur (back), and sloppy edges (feet).

BRUSHING FUR

Too fuzzy and "growing"
Here the fur angle is too perpendicular, the fur is too long, or you used too much GEL and paint. It happens!

Calm down! Monitor where your brush is going (not where it's been). Tighten up your strokes. Make corrections with clean brush drag-in strokes on the edge.

Too sleek The angle of the fur to the body is too shallow, the fur is too long and curled to the body contours, or you used excessive GEL. Any or all of these has made your animal look "greased down."

Lightly re-brush the edges with "popped-up" fur. Adjust the interior fur by layering and rotating it correctly. Like magic it's fluffy!

PAINT PROBLEMS

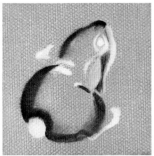

Immovable paint pattern Skimpy, too-turpy paint probably soaked through and stained the canvas (rather than floating on the background), or you rubbed the background too dry before painting.

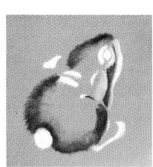

Try re-brushing with lots of GEL in a bristle brush with a scrubbing stroke. Then re-brush the fur to look pretty. (You may need more paint to make it look right.)

Snowplowed paint You used too much paint or didn't airplane the brush. This looks as if you skidded to a stop and all the paint piled up in front of you.

Re-brush some fur with drag-in strokes (cleaning your brush after each stroke). Then re-brush using airplane strokes, grabbing less paint from the edge in each stroke.

One-color fur Too much pressure on the brush mixed the various paint colors together.

Clean the brush often; use less pressure. Brush from light areas to dark instead of dark to light.

Wrong color fur You applied too much of one color, but you didn't realize it until you brushed the fur.

Don't worry! Lift out paint with a dry Q-Tip and re-brush with lots of GEL. Add fawn to fix Burnt Sienna stains.

GLOWING FUR

Disappearing glows You pulled too much paint into the turped Q-Tip highlight or didn't clean the brush often enough, letting the brush destroy the pinpoint-center white.

This is easy! Re-do the glow, but this time "sneak in" toward the center, never touching the pinpoint. Pull more color into the glow edges if needed. If your glow disappears again, just do it over until you get it!

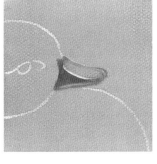

Mushy glows Not enough GEL was used in the brush (in proportion to the turp in the highlight) to stabilize the individual hair shapes.

Lift the glow out again, and re-brush with more GEL this time. Beautiful glows are a bit tricky, but you'll master it.

PAINTING TECHNIQUE

Bad blending and floating While blending, you stretched the colors too far one way, used heavy pressure on the brush, or over-mixed the paint. Unsuccessful floating of the white paint was caused by skimpy paint, or by too much pressure on the brush (which stirred up the previous paint layer).

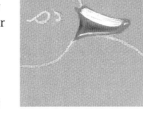

Technique is everything! Blend the line between the colors with a clean, dry brush, a feather touch, and a back-and-forth stroke. Float the white with a heavy load of soupy paint that falls off the brush easily. Same beak, but what a difference!

Paint skips Either your paint was too sticky, or you underloaded the brush. This always seems to happen when you least want it to.

It always pays to test your brush and paint load on a scrap piece of canvas. Use heavy loads of loose paint with no brush pressure, letting the paint flow off the brush.

BACKGROUNDS

Paint in the background This is the ultimate "Ooops!" but even this can be fixed. (Of course, it's better to prevent it by using a shield.)

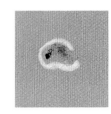  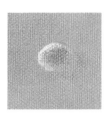

1 Lift out a ring around the mess, touching no part of it.

2 Remove the mess with a turped Q-Tip using a clean side for each stroke (stroke from the edge of the ring toward the center).

3 Mix some GEL into a bit of new background paint and re-apply with your finger. Smudge the area gently, and then smooth it with a paper towel. Repeat if necessary.

Unsuccessful backgrounds The usual causes are:
1. The proportion of turp, paint and GEL is incorrect.
2. The mix is sticky due to the turp evaporating.
3. You've used paper towels incorrectly.
4. Or a combination of all of these.

Keep practicing . . . and try these tips:
- Use a very pale color—it's easier.
- Use a plain background style (no halo).
- Use a 5″×7″ plain background. Most of the designs will fit, and there's less background to worry about.
- Use a cloudy or abstract-shape background style.
- Use white paint rather than raw canvas on the edges and fade it into the grey circle where the image will be.
- Invent your own style! As long as there is GEL and some color behind the animal, it will work!

USING ACRYLIC PAINT

Painting baby animals with acrylics is easy using the same basic techniques as for oils. Since acrylics dry rapidly, paint and finish only small areas of an animal before moving to an adjacent area. Substitute water for turp and use an acrylic gel medium such as FolkArt Blending Gel. Know that various brands of acrylic paint perform quite differently. FolkArt Artist's Pigments is a good choice. Replace sable brushes with good quality synthetic brushes such as Ruby Satin from Silverbrush, Ltd.

Special Tips
1. Add ⅓ generic glycerin emollient (from the drugstore) to gel medium used in the backgrounds to increase the open time up to several days.
2. Paint pure gel over the area of the design you are working on before beginning the paint pattern. Keep a small area painted with wet gel just ahead of where you are working to ensure a smooth transition to adjacent areas.
3. Redefine edge fur with a filbert grass comb for finer tips.
4. Replenish the gel on your bristle brush frequently when brushing fur.
5. Experiment glazing dry fur with gel and some paint on a filbert grass comb.

INDEX